SCALE

40 60 80 100

ATUTE MILES

LEGEND

S LOST WITH ENTIRE CREWS
S STRANDED TOTAL LOSS
S STRANDED SALVAGED

NORTH NO · NORTH · NORTH · 1ST
NORTH-WEST BY NORTH
NORTH-WEST
NORTH-WEST BY WEST
WEST NORTH-WEST
WEST BY NORTH
WEST
WEST BY SOUTH
WEST SOUTH-WEST
SOUTH-WEST BY WEST
SOUTH-WEST
SOUTH-WEST BY SOUTH
SOUTH SOUTH-WEST
SOUTH BY WEST
SOUTH
SOUTH BY EAST
SOUTH SOUTH-EAST
SOUTH-EAST BY SOUTH
SOUTH-EAST
SOUTH-EAST BY EAST
EAST SOUTH-EAST
EAST BY SOUTH
EAST
EAST BY NORTH
EAST NORTH-EAST
1ST · EAST

Georg J Hallw

INSON
YS RIVER

LAKE HURON

Georgian Bay

DEEPEST SOUNDING 720 FEET

ALPENA
ACADIAN
OHN A MC GEAN
PT.
ISAAC M SCOTT

AREA 23010 SQ. MILES

PTE. AUX BARQUES
NA JR MATOA
PT. CLARK
PORT AUSTIN
HARBOR BEACH
SAND BEACH
ARGUS
HYDRUS
D O MILLS GODERICH
JAMES CARRUTHERS
RT SANILAC
WEXFORD
REGINA ST. JOSEPH
PORT FRANKS
HEW ANDREWS NORTHERN QUEEN
YSTERY" SHIP THEDFORD
PORT HURON X H A HAWGOOD
SARNIA

ST. CLAIR RIVER

Lake St Clair

AREA 460 SQ. M.

OIT X
DETROIT RIVER
SOUTHEAST SHOAL
AREA 9940 SQ. MILES
LAKE ERIE
BAR PT.
LORAIN X CLEVELAND

J M JENKS
MIDLAND

COLLINGWOOD

C A N A D A

KINGSTON

AREA 7540 SQ. MILES

TORONTO X

LAKE ONTARIO

DEEPEST SOUNDING 774 FEET

HAMILTON
WELLAND CANAL X NIAGARA FALLS
LS 82 X BUFFALO

DEEPEST SOUNDING 210 FEET

A GREAT LAKES

X ERIE
CONNEAUT
ASHTABULA

LIGHTHOUSE

Chief Engineer Edward Sampson and Captain James B. Watts
of the steamer *J. F. Durston* with author Frank Barcus

FRESHWATER FURY

YARNS AND REMINISCENCES
OF THE GREATEST STORM
IN INLAND NAVIGATION

BY FRANK BARCUS

With maps and illustrations
by the author

DETROIT   WAYNE STATE UNIVERSITY PRESS   1960

Other publications by Frank Barcus

All Around Detroit—1939
Historic Michigan (pictorial map)—1954

Grateful acknowledgment is made to Prentiss M. Brown, to John B. Ford, Jr., and to the late Charles T. Fisher, Jr. for financial assistance in the publication of this volume.

*To the memory of the 251 sailors
who lost their lives while on duty
in the Great Storm of 1913.*

Foreword

THE GREAT LAKES have had too few historians. Frank Barcus is one of these historians. He singles out the bitter defeat inflicted by nature on the brave sailors of the Inland Seas, and his book is an important contribution to the Great Lakes story, graphically presented. Fortunately, Mr. Barcus wrote it while he was yet able to find and converse with many of the men who sailed those seas.

I can imagine the mariners of the Lakes reading this narrative in a single sitting, with a professional eye open for inaccuracies. They will find none, I predict. The rest of us will be absorbed by the sheer drama of it. This is all solid truth, and of its authenticity there is no question. That is what makes it rival, for excitement, the best maritime fiction of the ages.

> George W. Stark
> President, Detroit Historical
> Commission, and
> Historiographer, City of Detroit

Preface

THIS is strictly a sea story—a story of the fresh-water seas. Most sea tales are about the oceans, but the Great Lakes, too, have their historical lore. They have witnessed tragedies, adventures, and romances. They have their Flying Dutchmen. They have seen collisions and disasters and the sheer drama of the Great Storm of 1913.

Lest any reader think that this Storm was a tempest in a freshwater teapot, I give fair warning here and now that this book is about one of the grimmest storms on record. With its nightmare tragedies, it was the greatest disaster in the history of the Great Lakes.

Up and down the entire length of the Great Lakes, wherever men of the Lakes meet, whether on a back porch or in shipping circles, the Great Storm is still the topic of conversation. Tales, rumors, hearsay, suppositions are repeated—some true, some false, some overstated, some understated, but all with dramatic effect. The teller is always sure of an audience, for the story is never old. It is the greatest saga of the Great Lakes, and each man who survived the storm has his own version. The men who were in it will never forget the force of that wind, the blinding blizzard, the tumult of the seas, the staggering loss of lives and ships.

The Great Lakes are vital inland waterways. On their immense blue backs they carry the bread and iron of America. Over their surfaces moves the greatest flow of commerce the world has ever seen. The Lakes freighters can move three million tons of ore down from the upper ranges to the furnaces along the lower lakes in less than a week.

As a group, the Lakes form the largest body of freshwater seas in the world. Their water surface is more than 95,000 square miles, an area equal to the combined areas of the states of Michigan and Ohio. Singly each lake is an inland sea in itself, larger, more dangerous and with dirtier weather than many a sea better known in song and story. Lake Superior has all the majesty of the Pacific Ocean, Huron all the rugged restlessness of the Atlantic.

Superior, the mightiest lake of this cluster, has a length from Duluth to Point Iroquois of 383 miles, and a breadth of 160 miles. It is so large that a steamer can run for thirty hours in a direct course and never catch sight of land from either side of the ship. Its maximum recorded depth is 1,333 feet. Lake Michigan has a length of 321 miles and a breadth of 118; its maximum recorded depth is 923 feet.

The Great Lakes need ask no odds of any sea on earth when it comes to staging a hell-roaring storm in early winter. Their smashing seas can lift a helpless steel freighter as if it were a canoe and turn it over or set it broken on the shore. In the picturesque days of the sailing ships, the winds on the Great Lakes were known to have snapped off at their bases the masts of schooners—heavy columns of pine three feet or more thick at the deck and girded with iron—as if they were wooden matches.

Several of the ships sunk or pounded to pieces by the storm of 1913 were modern steel bulk freighters, from 440 to 550 feet in length and up to 7,862 gross tons. They were all staunch craft and ably commanded. They were considered the best products not only of the leading shipbuilders on the Lakes but of famous English and Scotch yards as well. Two of the steamers that disappeared with their entire crews, the *Wexford* and the *Leafield*, were typical English tramps, craftsmen-built to navigate any waters in the world.

To this day, the secret of why many of these fine freighters were among the missing remains buried at the bottom of the Lakes. Two weeks before the navigation season would have closed and the ships would have been safe in their winter berths, suddenly, practically without warning, the Great Storm sent a score of modern freighters to their doom. Twelve ships disappeared with their entire crews, leaving nothing behind to tell of their last battle with wind and sea. Eight of these were lost in the deadly pocket of Lake Huron, within a hundred miles of Port Huron, Michigan. Every veteran sailor on the Great Lakes will quickly recall them—The *Argus, Hydrus, Regina, Wexford, James*

Carruthers, John A. McGean, Isaac M. Scott, and the *Charles S. Price.* The most appalling tribute to the Storm's power was the toll it took in human life—over two hundred and fifty men.

The big lake carrier *Henry B. Smith* pulled out of Marquette and disappeared with all hands. The loss of the *James Carruthers,* a modern steel freighter, was incredible, and caused more technical criticism and discussion than that of any other ship, as she was considered the most modern and best constructed boat on the Lakes. The owners had sacrificed earning power for seaworthiness, adding extra tons of steel to her hull and thus diminishing her carrying capacity. She was 550 feet long, had a 58 foot beam and was of 7,862 gross tons. Besides those ships lost, fifty-one others, averaging three thousand tons each, were severely damaged, with a property loss of more than ten million dollars.

It is hard to visualize these great steel freighters being battered to pieces on the rocks by the mountainous waves towering above them. It is even harder to picture them overturned in the trough of the yawning seas or sinking in the vastness of the icy black waters. How much easier it is to picture the spacious calm of a summer day, when the water and the sky make a frame for the long picture ships bound north and south through the glassy stillness.

The authors and poets of the world have honored the salt water sailors but our freshwater sailors they have neglected. Our Great Lakes sailors are largely inarticulate and do not consider themselves heroic. Nor is there much romance in their make-up. They are hard workers who often place a higher value on duty than on life, a fact that will be shown in the following chapters. They are not endowed with the glamour of the ocean, but the ships they sail have been recognized for the vital job they perform. Their hardships and heroism may be overlooked, but national necessity has put a high price on continued operation of the Great Lakes fleet.

Here, then, is the complete tale, an historical record of the greatest storm on the Great Lakes. Here you will learn of the gallant struggle waged by the ships that were wrecked and the ships that were miraculously saved. My hope is that the tale will pass on to you at least some of the strength and magic of actuality.

All of the episodes recorded are factual, taken from the direct accounts of the men who survived the Great Storm. Much of the background material and many of these accounts are taken from the columns of the Detroit *News* and the Detroit *Free Press* for November 10–20, 1913, and November 12–15, 1940; from newspaper clippings in the scrapbooks of many captains and seamen on the long ships; and from the 1914 *Annual Report of the United States Life-Saving Service*.

Supplementary material and appendixes have been added from the *Monthly Weather Review* for November 1913, and from the 1913 *Annual Report of the Lake Carriers' Association*, Cleveland, Ohio. Where my sources disagreed on statistical matters, I have generally relied on the Association's figures.

Acknowledgment is made to the Michigan Historical Collection of the University of Michigan for permission to use the material in Chapter 13, and to *Inland Seas*, the quarterly journal of the Great Lakes Historical Society, for permission to use the material in Chapter 3.

I wish to express my appreciation to Dr. Fred Landon of London, Ontario, former vice-president of the University of Western Ontario and author of *Lake Huron*, for his careful reading of the manuscript and his helpful criticism. I am particularly indebted to him for some of the statistical information given in Appendix A. I also wish to thank Mrs. Georgiana W. Strickland for her editorial assistance and Dr. Harold A. Basilius for his valuable suggestions.

Frank Barcus

Introduction

I REMEMBER the Great Storm of 1913. I stood
on the shore of Lake Huron on Sunday, November 9, the third
day of the gale. The wind from the northwest was so strong that
one could lay full weight against it and stand as I did. The waves
were high and close together and it was cold. Hard nuggets of
frozen spray drove a hundred feet ashore. Late in the afternoon
the snow began and by the next morning fourteen inches had
fallen around the Straits of Mackinac. Had this storm occurred
in 1959, the air waves would have been filled with calls from
stricken ships. But in 1913, the air had not been harnessed for
communication. Men and ships were on their own. Everyone
around the Lakes—at Cleveland, Chicago, Duluth, Detroit—
knew that disaster had struck. But it was several days before news
of the tremendous loss of life and ships reached land and more
than a week before the full story was revealed. Even today,
mystery surrounds many a wreck. I will not transgress on Frank
Barcus' story by recounting the known details. They are well
told in the pages that follow.

When I first read *Freshwater Fury*, I knew at once that the
story must be preserved, lest with the passing years these vivid
tales would pale and be forgotten. Parts of this history have
been told by others in various books about the Lakes, but Mr.
Barcus has brought together in one volume the stories of the
sailors who faced the Great Storm and lived.

To those of us who live on the shores of the Great Lakes, the
story of the 1913 hurricane holds a solemn and a sad interest.
Each autumn, it seems, the brutal forces of nature gather to
remind men that the Lakes are unconquered. Men of science and
courageous sailors are still battling to conquer the elements. Brave
men still go down to the sea in ships.

Prentiss M. Brown

Contents

Illustrations

CHAPTER 1

The Gathering Storm

SOMEWHERE in the center of the Great Lakes area, an atmospheric depression formed, and from as far away as the barren Arctic, huge masses of air started to flow towards it. Thrown to one side by the rotation of the earth, these air masses traveled in a great regular curve, constantly increasing their speed as they swept down from the north. With the winds came a thick snow that swirled like an impenetrable white veil reducing visibility to a few feet.

The Arctic winds swept across Lakes Superior, Huron and Erie in a compact wall of icy air, and the sluggish waters, which had already begun to form into green ice, became agitated. At first the water rose and fell in rhythmic swells, but hardly had the first wave formed its smooth hillock, than its crest was torn and deformed by the rushing wind.

Thick and heavy, the water grew terrifying when lashed into action by the wind. Each heavy wave seemed more like lead than water—dull, dense, nearly solid. When its crest broke, instead of hissing into white, foamy spray, it fell in a single mass, like a sheet of some strange metal bending under its own weight. Thus began the Great Storm and the destruction of scores of ships across the expanse of the Great Lakes. A few ships would come through, battered but safe. Others would meet death within a few terrible hours. But all would be victims of one of nature's giant pranks.

The storm first made its presence known on Friday, November 7, 1913, as it centered over Minnesota. Because it was near to and heading for the Great Lakes region and probably would increase in energy as it moved eastward, the United States Weather Bureau telegraphed a storm warning to all stations on the Great Lakes:

HOIST SOUTHWEST STORM WARNINGS TEN A.M. . . . STORM OVER UPPER MISSISSIPPI VALLEY MOVING NORTHEAST. . . . BRISK TO HIGH SOUTHWEST WINDS THIS AFTERNOON AND TONIGHT SHIFTING TO NORTH-WEST SATURDAY ON UPPER LAKES. . . . WARNINGS ORDERED THROUGHOUT THE GREAT LAKES. . . .

Weather Bureau stations in all Great Lakes ports acted immediately on the warning and displayed the storm flags. At that time the Bureau was as much joked about by the sailors on the Lakes as was the Model T Ford by landlubbers. But navigators received no up-to-the-minute reports on the path of a storm, and for that reason, reliance on the Weather Bureau's predictions was of the utmost importance. Once caught out on the Lakes in a storm of hurricane proportions, there was no turning around or relying on sea room. Yet knowing all this, no one believed that this particular blow would develop into the storm it did. Time was too valuable to stop for storms. The only damaging evidence against the mariners, as Captain Robert Edelman points out, was that the warnings went unheeded.

"The ship I was aboard was loading ore in Ashland, Wisconsin, on that fateful day. I shall never forget it," recalls Captain Edelman, who was then first mate on a Lakes freighter. "The weather was sultry and the sky filled with dark oily-looking clouds. Before we were loaded, two red flags with square black centers were hoisted on a shore flag staff, indicating a storm.

"The crew began speculating whether the Old Man would take the ship out with these ominous red flags staring him in the face. We were worried and hoped he wouldn't. But what could we expect? The season was drawing to a close and he wanted to complete as many trips as possible before ice blocked the rivers.

"The dreaded order came: 'Take special care battening down the hatches.' We knew then we were going to sail, come hell or high water, and soon the boat was heading for the treacherous open lake."

The life of a storm warning is twenty-four hours unless it is ordered down previously by the forecaster. The warnings of Friday were to expire by limitation at 10:00 A.M. Saturday, unless extended by telegraph, or unless at the time of expiration the wind was still blowing with gale force.

During the daylight hours of Friday, the storm moved eastward to Marquette, where it centered Friday night. This was its expected path, known in weather circles as the northern circuit of the Lakes. From the end of this circuit, a storm usually takes its course directly across the St. Lawrence valley and right on to the Atlantic Ocean. The time generally allotted for this journey is between three and four days. This storm, however annoying it was, was still just another minor disturbance to the mariners. It continued its regular eastward movement during Friday night.

Saturday morning it was central near the Soo, lowest pressure 29.45. Rain was falling over Lakes Huron and Erie and northwest winds with snow prevailed over eastern Lake Superior. These winds were still not particularly dangerous. They reached a high of only thirty-eight miles an hour at Marquette. This, however, was sufficiently strong to warrant the continuation of the storm warnings. Nevertheless, to make sure, an order was telegraphed to all stations at 10:00 A.M. Saturday to continue the storm warnings, with an additional order to change the indicated wind direction from southwest to northwest. This automatically extended the life of the warnings to 10:00 A.M. Sunday.

As subsequent events proved, these storm warnings were fatally insufficient. They should have been a definite forecast for a hurricane—a warning that is almost never necessary on the Great Lakes.

During Saturday the storm changed its direction. Now it moved slowly southeastward from the Soo until at nightfall it was central in the vicinity of Alpena, Michigan. The wind velocity was forty-two miles. This was all within the expected course and the only disturbing factor from the forecaster's point of view was the fact that the barometric readings indicated considerably stronger winds than were actually being experienced.

The seas, in the meantime, had changed. To be sure, the waves had been whoppers before, like harmless giants who liked to worry the big freighters and who might conceivably do harm if one was careless. Now they were getting malicious. On Sunday, November 9, all the pent-up fury of the hurricane crashed down on the restless waters with murderous rage. Without warning, the body of the roaring storm tore across Lakes Huron and Erie. The seas became riotous, as if those giants had turned raving mad, tumbling about viciously to form mountains of moving dynamite. All day Sunday, throughout Sunday night, and most of Monday, the wind continued its deadly attack, blinding its victims with a smothering blanket of snow. All the country east of Chicago battled this ugly blizzard for more than forty hours. When snow was joined to the rising winds of Sunday, peril stalked the Lakes.

Ships whose masters had not seen or had ignored the storm warnings were now trapped between a vicious storm and a vicious shore, a desperate position indeed. The great and the small, the strong and the weak, were alike impotent before the assault. Both the most modern and the most ancient vessels were imperiled. All were soon at the mercy of wind and sea, for the blizzard blotted out the familiar landmarks, buoys, range lights, and other marine aids vital to safe navigation.

The highest and steadiest winds, with velocities just above ninety miles an hour, came between 6:00 and 10:00 P.M. Sunday, after the vessels had already been buffeted for hours. Ships were driven helplessly at the whim of the gale, some of the proudest and mightiest of them foundering in the hopeless smother. The men in those ships, men who gave speed and life to the inert hulls and motion to the quiet engines and roaring power to the boilers, died with their iron masters. No one knows what may have been their death struggles against the common enemy. To these at least came rest. To those who survived, even a moment's respite was impossible. For days and nights skippers kept their watch in the pilot house while the engine crews worked heroically in the bowels of the ships.

"It was an awful wild and raging sea," says Captain James Watts of the steamer *J. F. Durston,* veteran master in sail and steam. For seventy-two hours, without a moment's rest, Captain Watts stood watch, while his chief engineer, Edward Sampson, grimly stood the same trick below deck with his hand on the throttle. Those who hoped to survive could hardly do otherwise in the terrible wind and seas that were running.

"The waves broke over our bow with a thunderous force that was terrifying," Captain Watts continues, "crashing over us from both starboard and port. They met in the center of the deck and rushed wildly down the deck, hell bent for the engine house, breaking over it with a roar and a boom like hundreds of cannon. Then they curled up—often above the ridge of the smoke stack —and sped over the stern of the ship. It is absolutely impossible to imagine the terror of those waves. They were like mountains, and a glance into the trough from the pilot house was like looking far down into a seething valley during an upheaval of nature."

All the ships coming down the Lakes were swept by these mountainous waves. They tore away upper works or flooded the ships to a depth of several feet, at the same time sweeping overboard rigging, cabins, and pilot houses. The toughest sailor felt his stomach heave when he dared look down from the ship into the abyss of the trough.

The waves are reported to have run forty feet high in areas swept by the worst of the storm. The scientific explanation for the presence of such waves on the Great Lakes is that fresh water is lighter than salt water and is therefore more easily heaped up by a gale.

Lake Huron claimed the heaviest toll of human life. Its west shore (the State of Michigan), usually its weather shore, harbored scores of ships when the storm broke. This was a fatal mistake for many skippers. Unexpectedly, the wind shifted and the west shore received the full force of the mighty gale. The sailors' haven became the Great Lakes' biggest graveyard.

Next to Lake Huron, Lake Superior claimed the biggest toll of life and property. The storm on Superior was as severe as that on Huron but the wind did not shift, blowing steadily from the

northwest. Here the force of the wind snapped two-inch steel
mooring cables as if they were pieces of string.

On Lake Erie, the steamer *Calcite* was swept by a mighty black
wall of water rising skyward. On its top rode a rumbling white
crest that smashed the ship's rigging, skylights, life boats, and
all the windows in the pilot house. Captain Joseph Parsons
describes the approach of the great wave as having been pre-
ceded by a deep rumbling, heard for some time before the
wave itself could be seen.

On Lake Michigan, scores of ships were wrecked. The steamer
Black, while moored at her dock in Gary, had every one of her
windows torn out by the gale and was pounded into the concrete
pier until she was a complete wreck.

In Milwaukee harbor the entire south breakwater, under construction at the time, was swept away by the heavy seas with a
loss exceeding $100,000. Thousands braved the weather and cold
spray to witness this spectacle, something they had thought was
impossible. With the breakwater gone, the seas began demolishing
extensive improvements under way at South Park along the shore.
Chicago suffered a million-dollar loss in wrecked docks, washed-
out boulevards, uprooted trees, smashed plate glass windows and
wrecked telephone and telegraph lines. It was nothing short of
a miracle that scores of lives were not lost in the Chicago area
alone.

The storm ripped and smashed its way onward through Monday,
laying waste the country as savagely as an invading army. When
the end finally came, the story began to come out. Bit by bit,
as the storm eased off on Tuesday and began to dissipate its
strength in the St. Lawrence valley, the horror of what had
actually happened became clear to the stunned maritime world.
The grisly score was added up slowly and painfully. Actually,
it took weeks to learn the extent of the damage and to number
the missing, for the entire communications network was wrecked
by the storm.

The city of Cleveland and the Cleveland ship-owners bore the
brunt of the damage; the loss in the city itself amounted to more
than five million dollars. Telephone and telegraph lines for a
hundred miles around the city were destroyed. Whoever coined
the phrase "any port in a storm" could not have visualized the

destruction to all the ships in the Cleveland harbor when the storm struck.

"I have seen many storms in my day, but never one that wreaked the havoc this one did in Cleveland on Sunday and Monday," reminisced Mr. C. P. Staubach of Detroit, assistant sales manager of the Burroughs Adding Machine Company, who had passed through Cleveland on Tuesday on his way home from New York.

"All the way from Ashtabula to Cleveland the railroad tracks were blocked by telegraph poles and wires; the wires were tangled around them in one unholy mess. It was the same damned mess around every signal tower and station. Gangs of men were out ahead of us all day, chopping away the poles and clearing the railroad track for us. It took twelve hours to work the train through the city of Cleveland itself, a run which normally takes about twelve minutes. The station in Cleveland was packed with a solid mass of humanity—people who had sought refuge there or wanted to get a train out of town. Traffic in the city was completely suspended. The snow drifts were eight feet deep in the streets. Wires were down everywhere and people wouldn't cross the street for fear of being electrocuted."

The storm had struck as if it knew where it could do the most harm. Cleveland, paralyzed and cut off from the outside world, learned with bitter slowness that she had suffered the greatest portion of the loss and death, on the waters as well as at home. Twenty of the freighters that had disappeared or were stranded or pounded to pieces on the rocks were owned in Cleveland, and 186 men on those ships lost their lives.

The surviving vessels were counted slowly as they rode in anchorage or limped into home port. They were clearly crippled, ice-covered survivors who had been forced to fight it out. Most of them could hardly be recognized because of their ghostly mantles of heavy ice; they resembled miniature icebergs. All the doors to the deck houses and pilot houses were so tightly sealed that they had to be chopped or steamed open.

Other steamers were heard from as they lay stranded on the beach or caught on the rocks to which the Storm had driven them, and where they were pounded by the seas while frantic rescue workers toiled to save the men aboard.

At 2:00 A.M. Sunday, the first casualty of the Storm was reported. The old wooden steamer *Louisiana* was blown aground on Washington Island, Lake Michigan, near Green Bay. Then harrowing tales started coming in—tales of trapped vessels being pounded for hours, some even for days, by seas which made rescue impossible.

Now, for hundreds, came agonizing days of waiting for news that never came—news of ships that were never seen again. The first discoveries of wreckage and bodies told only part of the story. Then, for many, came the worst agony of all—the hope against hope, that somehow, someway, one precious life had been spared. But not a single seaman survived the foundered ships; no man could have. And but two small voices ever came from the depths, one an anguished note enclosed in a bottle and the other a message on a door panel washed up on the shore of Lake Erie.

Many stories will never be known. The mystery of an overturned steamer was finally cleared up, at least as far as her identity was concerned. But no one knows how the storm overturned her. And forever lost is the answer to the riddle of two bodies washed ashore in each other's arms—the bodies of men from two different ships.

Although the vital statistics were soon on paper and the damage written off, the Great Storm is still alive in the memories of the men who survived it. The old sailors say its equal in fury will probably never be met on the Great Lakes again.

CHAPTER 2

The Storm's First Casualties

BEFORE the Great Storm had reached its full force, while rural telegraph lines were still intact, the news of the first casualty slipped through to the world when a rescued sailor tried to send a message to his wife. Even as the message was being clicked out, the wire went down and all that got through were the words, "LOUISIANA WRECKED ON WASHINGTON ISLAND. . . ." The *Louisiana,* bound from Milwaukee for Alpena, light, was blown into Green Bay by the Storm. "At 12:15 A.M. Sunday," according to first mate Finley McLean, "the brisk wind died out almost completely; yet in less than half an hour we were fighting for our lives in a fifty-five mile gale that tore upon us from the nor'west.

"We tried to drop the anchor to escape being blown on the beach, but the wind was too much for us. It blew us back faster and faster and all this time the engines were going full steam

9

ahead. By 1:00 A.M., the wind had increased to seventy miles an hour and we were really scared. We were fighting helplessly to keep off the beach. We just couldn't do a damn thing. At 2:00 A.M., we struck the shore on Washington Island.

"Our situation then was even more terrible. The wind and seas were breaking over the entire ship. Six hours later we finally managed to get a man ashore to take the news of the wreck to the lifesavers at Plum Island.

"Before he even reached there, we were placed in deadly peril and were forced to face the icy breakers. How it happened we never knew for certain, but the old *Louisiana* caught fire. Probably the wrecked engines started it, but we never had a chance to find out. The old craft was made of wood and burned like tinder.

"Fighting the blaze was hopeless. We launched a lifeboat as fast as possible into the roaring breakers and floundered through them safely to shore, half drowned, two-thirds frozen, and just blamed scared. We were smart to start so promptly. In fifteen minutes from the start of the blaze, the whole ship was wrapped in flames. She burned clear to the water as we watched. There was nothing left of her but her red-hot engines, which hissed like a volcano and sent off clouds of steam as the seas rushed over them.

"We turned away from the *Louisiana's* graveyard and started to make our way to shelter. The nearest house, we found out later, was five miles away on the other side of miles of snowdrifts, many of which were over our heads. We discovered a novel but very effective way of getting through the drifts. Since I was the smallest man in the crew, they chose me for the trail-breaker. The big men would pick me up, then after a good swing would throw me against a snowbank, and crawl in after me. I didn't like this chilly trick any too well, you can bet. But in this manner we finally made our way to a snow-hidden farmer's house, where we got dry clothes and food and a chance to thaw out.

"I was anxious to notify my wife, so that if she got news of the wreck from other sources she wouldn't worry about me. At the first opportunity I made my way to a telegraph station on the island where I managed to get a message started. I wasn't quick enough, however, for the wire went down as my message was being transmitted, breaking all contact with the outside world. All the receiving end ever got were the words 'LOUISIANA WRECKED ON WASHINGTON ISLAND.' Fortunately the operator knew or guessed the purpose of the message and mercifully added the word 'SAVED.' It was Tuesday before we could get to the first town on the mainland, Escanaba. Until I sent her further word from there, my wife hardly slept at all.

"That storm was the worst I had ever seen in ten years of sailing. The blizzard of 1905 couldn't compare with it. And I should know, for in 1905 I was in the *Fleetwood,* which was hurled about for three days and nights and finally driven into Marquette with more than ten feet of water in her hold."

The brave seaman who had left the *Louisiana* to report her situation to the Plum Island Lifesaving Station had carried out his orders. As the lifesavers were hurrying overland with their boat, they learned of the *Louisiana's* burning, and that the crew had escaped. There was, of course, nothing to be done for the *Louisiana*. She had died as if from a sudden stroke.

As the lifesavers were returning to their station, they received a report that the barge *Halsted* was in a dangerous position only a hundred yards or so from the very spot where the *Louisiana's* men had landed shortly before. Tired as the lifesavers were, they did what must be done while the opportunity was still theirs. They immediately pressed on through the snowdrifts to the aid of the *Halsted*. They found her battling the waves about three-quarters of a mile from the harbor entrance, dragging her anchors, as yet not within reach. They had stubbornly pulled their boat and beach equipment with them, but no open boat could have survived the gale blowing then. There was nothing they could do but wait until the vessel was near enough shore to be reached with a life line.

The shoreward progress of the *Halsted* was slow but steady. The lifesavers anxiously kept tab on her performance. As she was being driven inland, her anchors would suddenly fetch her up, holding her for an hour or more, a victim of the battering seas and wind. Then an increase in the wind would set her anchors dragging again. For twenty hours, the Plum Island lifesavers kept their frozen watch on the rocky reefs, while inch by inch the *Halsted* worked steadily on to her destruction.

By 5:00 A.M. Monday, she had been blown to within sixty feet of the dangerous shore. When the ship struck a huge rock, the lifesavers immediately went into action. Working in the bitter cold, they soon got a whipline aboard with the help of the seven crewmen. Everything was in the proper position for the use of the breeches-buoy.

But the brave and devoted Plum Island men were unexpectedly cheated of their triumph over the storm, their moment to prove themselves. As they were about to send the canvas breeches to the stranded and frozen seamen for the first rescue, the sea suddenly lifted the *Halsted* lightly from the rocks and brought her crashing down so close to land that her wet and frozen crew was able to climb down a rope ladder to the top of a large flat rock. The wind had moderated slightly by 3:00 P.M., so the Plum Island men started back to their station, arriving near noon on Tuesday. Two days of exposure to a sixty-mile gale and arctic temperatures left the men cold, hungry, and utterly exhausted.

The landsman who reads this incident may find it grimly amusing. He may picture the disappointed lifesavers returning dejected from what they had fondly hoped would be a thrilling rescue, complete with medals and the grateful kisses of beautiful captains' daughters. There were many thrilling rescues over that weekend, some of which you will read more about. But the Life-saving Service wasn't paid to be glamorous. It was there when needed and most of its work was hard and dangerous. The Service was built on what most of its men did and not on the spectacular achievements of a few, no matter how proudly the Service itself and the rest of the world may look upon its most thrilling and glorious moments.

Take the case of the British steamer *Acadian*, stranded on a reef a mile off Sulphur Island in Thunder Bay, Lake Huron, on a trip from Kingston to Fort William, Ontario. Because of the blinding blizzard on Sunday, she was not discovered on the rocks until the next afternoon. When the message reached the Thunder Bay Lifesaving Station, ten miles from the scene of the stranding, it said that, since the weather had moderated some, the services of the lifesaving crew would not be needed. On Tuesday, however, the Storm increased and the master requested the standby services of the lifesaving crew. They set out immediately in their thirty-four foot power lifeboat. For several days and nights they kept a close watch on the ship's reaction to the breakers and assisted the crew in their desperate attempts to save vessel and cargo. Completely exhausted by strain and fatigue, their fingers torn, raw and bleeding from throwing cement from the hold into the lake, the lifesaving corps returned to its station six days later for a well earned rest.

On the nineteenth, the *Acadian* was floated and towed to Alpena. Several hundred tons of cement had been thrown overboard and about the same weight of cargo had been lightered. The damage sustained and the loss in cargo amounted to nearly 50 percent of the value of both ship and cargo, which was reported to have been $325,000.

This was hardly the thrilling rescue work that writers like to tell about, but it was, nevertheless, hard work and dangerous and very necessary. Going out in mountainous seas in open boats is never without risk, enough risk to give even veteran sailors pause, but it is a risk which the lifesavers must always take when it's humanly possible. The story of Captain McLeod of the *Matoa* bears this out.

The *Matoa* was bound from Toledo, Ohio, to Hancock, Michigan, with a cargo of soft coal. The vessel had made its way up Lake Huron with little trouble, passing Port Huron at 12:30 Sunday morning, then Harbor Beach four hours later. At 6:20 A.M., about opposite Sturgeon Point and well out in the lake, the first of the heavy seas struck her, without warning, and the heavy curtain of snow soon cut off everything from sight.

"The seas broke in a smother of foam over the decks," says Captain McLeod, "and before we knew what had happened they stove in part of the after cabin, flooded the messroom and kitchen and let a mountain of water into the engine room. They carried away three hatch strong-backs.

"The waves were so bad we had to turn and run before the wind. How we dreaded the thought of attempting this turn. We prepared for this dangerous maneuver by pouring a barrel of oil over each bow. I believe that saved us from shipping a deadly mass of water during the four minutes it took to turn.

"We steered south by east, turning over our engines at twenty-six to the minute. Ice was forming rapidly in the fifteen-degree cold. To our great relief, the ship showed every sign of lasting it out in spite of the terrific battering she was taking, but at 10:00 P.M., we received a vague sensation of impending disaster. We were right. The sixteen hours of continual strain proved too much. She started to crack up before our eyes. A spar deck plate just forward of the boiler house on the starboard side split open, leaving a gap which extended the full width of the plate.

"For a short while nothing else went, but about midnight, just as we were praying and hoping and beginning to breathe a little easier, a bigger mountain than any of the others overtook us astern and smashed in the after cabin. It looked bad. Anything might happen at any instant, for the force of the water made a bulge of about three feet in the bulkhead between the engine room and dining room, leaving this battered bulkhead, already structurally punished, as the only protection between the engine room and the sea.

"Everything considered, perhaps it's lucky that we stranded at 12:30 A.M. Monday. This happened about two miles east of the Pointe Aux Barques Lifesaving Station and about the same distance off shore. After stranding she ran about a thousand feet before she stopped. She was heading south by west one-half west, with about eighteen feet of water under her stern and fourteen feet under her bow. She swung two points to the west after she struck.

"The condition of the after cabin was such that if we had been in deeper water the ship wouldn't have stayed afloat for more than a half an hour after she struck, for her engine room would certainly have been filled with water coming through the after partition."

The distress signals blown by the *Matoa* after she struck were heard by the lifesaving station lookout and were immediately answered by a pyrotechnic signal known as a Coston flare. But because of the mountainous seas and the force of the wind, the lifesavers could not go immediately to the rescue. The water, which had risen four to five feet above its normal level, was sweeping through the station boathouse in massive surges. The boathouse doors were already smashed in and the launchways were destroyed. The building that housed the power lifeboat had been torn from its foundations and the boat and carriage had been thrown completely off track. Even the solid concrete breakwater which afforded protection for the launching of lifeboats had been swept away like so many pebbles. The lifesavers themselves were helpless and in no position to help others. It was not until Tuesday morning that they succeeded, despite difficulty, in putting off to the *Matoa* in their surfboat.

Meanwhile, the members of the *Matoa* crew were making the best of it in spite of their unhappy position. "When she struck," says Captain McLeod, "all the crew who were aft got forward and with the aid of oil heaters all hands kept fairly comfortable until daylight. The after cabin, boiler house, lifeboats, funnels and the rest of the upper works were a mass of ice.

"Soon after daylight, the sea moderated enough so that some of the crew could go aft and get a small coal stove, which they set up in the windlass room, and for the rest of the time we were in the boat this gave us sufficient heat to keep quite comfortable."

On Tuesday morning, the lifesavers arrived alongside the *Matoa* in their surfboat. They found her crew all safe on board. The surfboat, as it stood by the stranded vessel, looked like a peanut on the storm-tossed ocean and failed to impress the seamen as a likely means of escape. One and all, they preferred to take their chances on the reef rather than trust their lives to the tossing cockleshell in which the surfmen were so nonchalantly riding the waves. It looked to the *Matoa*'s crew like a jump from the frying-pan into the fire. "The whole damn crew, to a man, refused to take *that* little joyride," an engineer said afterwards. The lifesavers, therefore, returned to their station, taking only requests for a tug, lighter, air compressors and, last but not least, provisions.

On Wednesday morning, the wrecking tug *Favorite* arrived and began unloading the *Matoa*'s cargo of coal. After she had worked at the wreck for two days, the high seas at last forced her to pull up anchor and run for shelter in the harbor, taking the crew of the *Matoa* with her.

The refusal of the *Matoa*'s men to be rescued was unusual but not unique in the history of the Great Storm. The crew of the stranded steamer *D. O. Mills* did even better—or worse. They completely ignored the men who risked their lives to rescue them.

Shortly after 11:00 P.M. Sunday, the *Mills* was driven hard and fast onto a reef half a mile off shore at Harbor Beach, Lake Huron. She was discovered at about 6:00 the next morning between snow squalls. No distress signals, if she made any, were seen or heard at the lifesaving station. Nevertheless, the lifesavers' duty was to make sure that the vessel was not in trouble; so, regardless of gale or seas, the Harbor Beach crew went out to investigate in their thirty-four foot power lifeboat. They found the *Mills* lying with her bow in the breakers, apparently full of water and resting solidly on the bottom. Around her they went, looking for any signs of distress or for any other signal at all, but none came. History doth not record how the eighteen crew members were improving their shining hours at that time, apparently without watch or worry; but the complete ignoring of both danger and rescue would seem to point to either a deep and dreamless sleep or a mighty absorbing crap game. There was nothing for the would-be rescuers to do but return to their station. The next morning the crew of the steamer pumped her out and, with the help of the heavy swells, worked off the reef. They took her under her own power to a drydock for repairs. She had suffered damage to the amount of $45,000, but fortunately, since she was light, there was no cargo loss involved.

It was all in a day's work for the Lifesaving Service. They had done their duty and were satisfied. Other crews risked their lives more spectacularly, in some cases tipping the fine balance between life and death; but in every instance the result was the same—whether emergency or routine, the job was done.

CHAPTER 3

The Sheadle *Dares the Deadly Trough*

W HATEVER descriptive powers or historical sources an author may have, his account can never have the immediacy, the reality, of an eye-witness story. Only someone who was there can really introduce you to the facts. No account of the Storm is so complete and detailed as that of Captain S. A. Lyons of the steamer *J. H. Sheadle.* He was within touching distance of death during the storm, fighting it from its beginnings in Lake Superior through to its wildest height in the fatal pocket of Lake Huron. No other skipper drove his ship south from the Soo that day and lived to tell of it. His report to the Cleveland-Cliffs Iron Company on the handling of his ship is the straightforward story of a courageous man.

The narrative and letter that follow were a gift of the captain's son, Mr. K. T. Lyons of Cleveland, to the Wakefield Museum of the Great Lakes Historical Society at Vermilion, Ohio, and were

published by the Society in *Inland Seas,* Spring 1956. Captain
Lyons' account reads:

"We loaded grain at Fort William and left there at 8:00 P.M.
the night of November 6. The captain of the *James Carruthers* and
I were in the shipping office together and intended to come down
together as we were going to get away at about the same time,
but evidently he did not get out until some time after I did.

"When I left the barometer was below normal but stationary,
and the wind had been blowing for some time. After getting outside of Thunder Cape [about fifteen miles from Fort William and
coming into Lake Superior] a heavy sea was running from the
southwest, and a strong breeze. I went back under Pie Island,
letting go anchor at 10:00 o'clock and lying there until 3:30 the
morning of the seventh, when the wind went north and we proceeded on our voyage.

"On arriving at Whitefish Bay it shut in very thick and foggy,
which held us there the balance of the night and until about 8:00
o'clock the following morning, November 8.

"There were a number of steamers lying at anchor further down
the bay and they, of course, locked down ahead of the *Sheadle.*
The *James Carruthers* locked down just ahead of us, then we followed at 8:30 P.M., with the *Hydrus* immediately after us, both
of which vessels were lost. It had been snowing, having commenced along in the afternoon. It was snowing some while we
were in the lock but had cleared up when we left the lock.

"I had wired the office I would not leave, but as it cleared up
we continued on down the river, passing out into Lake Huron at
1:53 A.M. the morning of November 9, with the wind light north-
northeast. The only variation in our course from that time until
practically within two miles of Thunder Bay was one-eighth of
a point. As we approached the fuel dock of Messrs. Pickands,
Mather and Co., we sighted the *Carruthers* taking fuel; she left
the dock, rounded to, and entered Lake Huron shortly before we
did.

"Before we arrived at Presque Isle, Lake Huron, it commenced
to snow some; sometimes it would clear up so that we could pick
up the land; we saw Presque Isle, Middle Island, and Thunder
Bay. From our soundings when we got to Thunder Bay at 8:35
A.M. we were about two miles outside of our regular course down

WHITEFISH BAY
From PORT WILLIAM
LOCKED DOWN
8.30 P.M. NOV 8
SOO LOCKS (SAULT STE. MARIE)
ST. MARYS RIVER

STRAITS OF MACKINAC
ENTERED LAKE HURON
1:53 A.M. NOV. 9
SPECTACLE REEF
POE REEF
MACKINAW CITY

GEORGIAN BAY

FALSE PRESQUE ISLE
MIDDLE ISLE
PRESQUE ISLE
WIND N.N.E STRONG

THUNDER BAY
8:35 A.M.
10 A.M.
SIX FATHOM BANK
11:30 A.M.

SCALE
0   10   50
STATUTE MILES

PORT AUSTIN REEF
POINTE AUX BARQUES
4:50 P.M.

SAGINAW BAY
HARBOR BEACH
GOODRICH

FURY STRIKES
5:45 P.M.
SECOND TURN
4:15 A.M. NOV. 10

FOURTH TURN
8:30 A.M. NOV 10
THIRD TURN
6:45 A.M.
FIRST TURN
10 P.M. NOV. 9

FORT GRATIOT
PORT HURON   SARNIA
ST. CLAIR RIVER

Approximate
TRACK *and*
TIME POSITIONS
of the steamer
J. H. SHEADLE
S. A. Lyons, MASTER.
During the Great Storm
on the GREAT LAKES
NOV. 9, 1913

LAKE ST. CLAIR

Lake Huron, having steered southeast by south one-eighth south. The barometer at this time was below normal, but stationary.

"In an hour and a half after passing Thunder Bay Island the wind had increased and there was a strong wind from north-northeast with snow. The sea kept on increasing, the wind changed to due north blowing a gale. At 11:30 A.M. the course was changed to south by east one-half east in order to bring the ship more before the sea, and we continued to shift from a half to a point as the sea increased so as to keep the ship running practically dead before it; also to keep the ship from rolling and the seas from breaking over the decks.

"We got the regular soundings at Pointe Aux Barques that we had been getting on previous trips, and by the soundings and the time we could tell when we were abreast of the point. It was snowing a blinding blizzard and we could not see anything. According to the soundings we got by the deep sea sounding lead we were abreast of Harbor Beach at 4:50 P.M. and three miles outside of the regular course we take during the summer. At this time the wind was due north and at Harbor Beach we changed our course to due south, running dead before the sea and wind.

"The bell rang for supper at 5:45 P.M., which was prepared and tables set, when a gigantic sea mounted our stern, flooding the fantail, sending torrents of water through the passageways on each side of the cabin, concaving the cabin, breaking the windows in the after cabin, washing our provisions out of the refrigerator and practically destroying them all, leaving us with one ham and a few potatoes. We had no tea or coffee. Our flour was turned into dough. The supper was swept off the tables and all the dishes smashed.

"Volumes of water came down on the engine through the upper skylights, and at times there were from four to six feet of water in the cabin. Considerable damage was done to the interior of the cabin and fixtures. The after steel bulkhead of the cabin was buckled. All the skylights and windows were broken in. A small working boat on the top of the after cabin and the mate's chadburn were washed away.

"It was blowing about seventy miles an hour at this time, with high seas, one wave following another very closely. Owing to the sudden force of the wind the seas had not lengthened out as they usually do when the wind increases in the ordinary way. In about four hours the wind had come up from twenty-five to seventy-five miles an hour, but I do not think exceeded seventy miles an hour.

"Immediately after the first sea swept over our stern, I ordered the boatswain to take sufficient men and shutters to close all windows in the after cabin. The men forced their way aft, braving the wind, sleet and seas, one hand grasping the life rail and the other the shutters. Reaching the after cabin in safety they began securing the shutters, when another tremendous sea swept over the vessel carrying away the shutters. The men were forced to cling to whatever was nearest them to keep from being washed overboard; immediately a third sea, equally as severe, boarded the vessel, flooding the fantail and hurricane deck. The men attempted to reach the crew's dining room but could not make it, and only saved themselves by gripping the nearest object they could reach. Indeed one of the wheelsmen was only saved from going over by accidently falling as he endeavored to grope his way to the rail, his foot catching in one of the bulwark braces, preventing him from being swept off. Another monster sea boarded the boat, tearing the man loose from the brace, and landing him in the after tow line which had been washed from its rack and was fouled on deck.

"The men finally made the shelter of the dining room and galley. One of the oilers stood watch at the dining room door, closing it when the boat shipped a sea and opening it when the decks were clear to let the water out of the cabins.

"The steward and his wife were standing knee deep in the icy water. The steward's wife was assisted into the engine room, the steward remaining in the dining room, securing furniture and silverware. The firemen and seamen were comfortable in their rooms as they were not touched. Some of the outfit of the private dining room was washed into the mess room, the steward's trunk was washed out of his room and stood on end in the galley. The steward's wife had to remain all night in the engine room wrapped in a blanket.

"Water through the engine room skylight drenched the two engineers who were throttling the engines; I do not think it ever happened before when these two men had to stand by those two positions constantly. From 2:30 P.M. until 5:00 the engines raced,

requiring the greatest care and judgment. At times the ship was
so heavily burdened with seas coming over her decks that her
revolutions were decreased from seventy-five to thirty-five turns
per minute. The engineers made their positions more comfortable
by rigging up a piece of canvas over the engines.

"We continued on our course, following our deep sea soundings, and at 9:00 o'clock had soundings of eighteen fathoms. This
carried us well off to the west shore. I called the engineer up at
this time and told him that at 10:00 o'clock (the night of November 9) I was going to turn around head to the sea unless I could
locate the land or Fort Gratiot light, and wanted to increase the
speed of the ship up to that time so as to enable me to bring the
boat around head to on account of the sea running behind us. At
10:00 o'clock we turned, heading north half east; the vessel rolled
very heavily but came around all right head to. I should judge that
we were ten minutes turning. At that time we were about ten
miles north of Fort Gratiot by the soundings we got—ten fathoms.
I had everything lashed before we turned. No one thought of a
life preserver. The way the ship was behaving we had every confidence in her. The heavy rolling tore adrift the binnacle on top
of the pilot house. After that it was extremely dangerous to be
in the house as this heavy object was hurled back and forth across
the deck as the ship labored and rolled in the heavy sea.

"During this time from Pointe Aux Barques to the foot of the
lake our log line iced heavily, and the seas at times washed brace
and dial inboard over the rail, rendering it useless. We were
obliged to depend entirely on the deep sea lead, which was in constant use for seventy hours, at half hour and fifteen minute intervals. By the use of the deep sea lead we knew where the ship
was at all times. Having the familiar soundings right along through
it all was the only thing that kept us from being wrecked, as it
gave us confidence as to our location. The men were familiar
with the use of the lead, as we had used the machine constantly,
but it was a great punishment on them to keep it going at this
time.

"Just after turning I sent the first mate aft to inspect the wheel
chains and quadrant. He telephoned me that they were all right
but that he could not get forward again at that time, the seas
covering the decks with a solid mass of blue water. The men of the

second watch had remained on deck with us, and while we would not let one man go aft alone we did not hesitate to let two go together.

"The mate made quite a fight to get forward but was unable to make it then, and crawled back to the engine room half conscious.

"I started back on a vice versa course, which would be north half east for six and one-quarter hours, following my soundings back from ten to twenty-two fathoms. During this time one of the wheelsmen got aft, securing a few pieces of bread, and came forward again with the mate and boatswain. One watchman remained on watch in the galley.

"At 5:15 A.M., November 10, I turned again, heading south one quarter west. This time we experienced much difficulty in turning, the ship remaining longer in the trough of the sea on account of not getting so much way and running head into it, but she behaved well, handled well in every way and steered well. The rolling was very bad—I was lifted right off my feet. Only by the greatest effort were the second mate and myself able to hold onto the stanchions on the top house, our legs being parallel with the deck most of the time.

"Again and again she plunged forward, only to be baffled in her attempts to run before it, sometimes fetching up standing and trembling from stem to stern. She was buffeted about by the tremendous seas, almost helpless, dipping her hatches in the water on either side, barrels of oil and paint getting adrift and smashing out the sides of the paint locker. The men were tossed around the wheel house at will.

"I feared her steering gear had given way, but fortunately on examination it proved to be all right. She would gain a half point, only to lose it, but finally after a mighty effort she swung around. I never had seen seas form as they did at this time; they were large and seemed to run in series, one mounting the other like a mighty barrier.

"Running back we decreased our speed from 'Full' to fifty-five turns as we got down closer to the river, following back on somewhat different soundings than we got going up. We came back in two hours where it took us six and one quarter to face the sea.

"At 6:30 A.M., November 10, I called the engineer and told him

I was not satisfied with the soundings we were getting, and to be prepared at any moment to give me full power to turn the ship again. We could see nothing on account of the heavy fall of snow.

"At 6:45 A.M. we turned for the third time, headed north by west. This time the sea had decreased, and the wind had gone to the northwest in the meantime, so that there was practically no sea to bother us any.

"The seventy mile gale lasted from about 10:00 o'clock Sunday morning until about 2:00 o'clock Monday morning, sixteen hours of it, with continuous snow all the time. We kept our whistle blowing all the time, but at times we up forward could not hear it ourselves.

"At 8:30 A.M. it had cleared up so we could see quite a distance, so we turned around again heading south one-half west, the wind and sea going down. In fifteen minutes we could see the west shore, and sighted what I suppose was the wreck of the *Price*, passing this hull at about a distance of 1,000 feet. We noted what we thought were oil barrels and wreckage floating not over a quarter of a mile to the leeward of her. Just before we arrived abreast of the wreck we cast our deep sea lead to determine what water there was in that locality, and found ten fathoms.

"We proceeded on our way over to the location where the Fort Gratiot lightship should have been stationed. We had slowed down to slow speed some time before we got in this locality. I picked up the stack of the lightship, which had drifted two or three miles out of position. Just at this time it shut in to snow again, and I backed away from the stack three-quarters of a mile or more, letting go my anchor, and waiting there until it cleared up at 12:00 o'clock noon.

"When it cleared up we proceeded on our voyage down, passing Detroit at 7:00 o'clock the evening of the tenth. After entering the river the steward served dinner in the galley, which was the first regular meal since Sunday noon, and which consisted of beef and potatoes. Supper was also served in the galley, consisting of ham and potatoes.

"The water being low, and we having no provisions, I tied up at Smith's coal dock to take provisions on board the next morning, the eleventh, leaving there at 9:00 o'clock when the water came up.

"When we arrived at Bar Point the water was unusually low and we grounded there in the west channel. We released ourselves with our own power after some five and a half hours' delay, getting on our way and proceeding on our voyage to Erie, that being our port of destination, where we arrived at 11:10 A.M., November 12."

STEAMER J. H. SHEADLE

Ann Arbor, Dec. 24, 1913

Mr. J. H. Sheadle, Secretary
The Cleveland-Cliffs Iron Co.
Cleveland, Ohio

Dear Sir:

Your letter received referring to my statement of the last trip, asking for my reasons for turning around three times during the storm of November 7, 8, and 9.

The first time, I turned around at the lower end of Lake Huron owing to the circumstances. I did not consider it safe to proceed any further on our course toward the river, or get in the locality where downbound steamers would likely be at anchor. From the soundings I felt perfectly safe in turning as I did. I had figured for some time previous on doing so, and had given the engineer ample time to be in readiness at such a time to turn around, which we did at the exact time and I have every reason to believe in the locality I had figured on.

You may ask the question why I did not let go my anchors after turning around under such conditions. I did not consider it a safe policy to do so, for had I attempted it there was a long chance of losing them, and at the same time putting the steamer in a position where it would be impossible to handle her. In fact, it has always been my policy not to try to find a harbor or anchorage under such conditions as long as my boat is seaworthy and is acting satisfactorily in every way.

The second time I turned, I figured I was far enough from the river to get back shortly after daylight, and besides I was not going that way with my cargo. I had also given the engineer due notice in regard to time, etc. Of course, we would naturally expect a little more difficulty in turning this time, but by the proper handling of the engines and the helm we turned around and headed back for the river.

The third time we turned there was no sea to speak of and we had no difficulty whatever in turning. The soundings were not satisfactory, and it was still snowing so that we could see no distance, and I did not consider it safe to proceed any further, especially as the soundings I had been getting were not satisfactory. I considered it policy to keep in good water until it cleared up.

About ten minutes after turning the last time it began to clear up so we could make out the shore line on both sides of the lake.

As to the question of the safety of the steamer other than stranding or collision, I considered her perfectly safe, as we had only run our ballast pump five hours in the twenty-four, and one-half of this time was taken up pumping out the weather side. After covering up the vent pipes on deck leading to the ballast tanks we had very little pumping to do.

At 11:00 A.M. on the ninth I called up the engineer and told him to start the ballast pumps on the weather side, and at 1:30 P.M. he called me and said they had a suck on all tanks on that side, and from that time on we only pumped two and a half hours during the bad weather.

I can truthfully say to you that at no time during this storm did I have any fear whatever for the safety of the steamer, and if any of my crew thought differently their actions did not show it.

Trust this explanation as to why I turned will be satisfactory to you.

Yours very truly,
S. A. Lyons

And so ends the story from the pen of Captain Lyons.

Very close to miraculous indeed was the *Sheadle's* survival. The waters through which she passed had proved fatal to many more ships then the overturned steamer that Captain Lyons had sighted, the famous mystery ship, and still more had been forced onto the rocks and beaches. There were ships besides the *Sheadle* that survived the storm, but none that followed through in a southward course on Lake Huron from beginning to end so closely in the heart of the fury.

CHAPTER 4

Smashing Through with the Durston

WHILE Captain Lyons was the only skipper to bring his ship down Lake Huron from the Soo during the Storm, Captain James B. Watts was the only skipper to take his ship, the *J. F. Durston,* straight on her northward course up Lake Huron, plowing right through the worst of the fury, fighting it out toe to toe with his mighty antagonist.

He brought his ship safely into port with her full crew and cargo, but for forty solid hours he and his crew of thirty-two stood with one hand on a lifeline and the other on the doorknob of Davey Jones's locker. While eight large modern steel freighters sank or turned turtle around them, Captain Watts, like Captain Lyons, kept the *Durston*'s nose right into the teeth of the Storm and plunged along as best he could until he brought her safely into Mackinaw.

"At any time from 5:00 P.M. Sunday, until after midnight," recalls Captain Watts, "we would have met our doom had the *Durston* got into the trough of those waves. We couldn't have lasted five minutes.

"In my experience with steamers, I have found it a good policy always to handle them the same as sailing vessels in bad weather —check them down and head into it or run before the seas. We happened to be going up, so, by heaven, we headed into it."

Few men were better qualified than Captain Watts to outface the fury of such a storm. He had the courage of his convictions and the experience to back them up. When he retired in 1930 as skipper of the *Stephenson,* he could look back on more than fifty crowded, exciting years of sailing the Great Lakes "man and boy, sail and steam, hand and master." He was the Ancient Mariner of the Great Lakes with tales that burned to be told.

Born in Collingwood, Ontario, he was but a lad of thirteen when he first sailed with his father. Two years later he took to the boats for good. There could be no other choice for the son of Matthew Watts, who, when his ship broke up in Lake Winnipeg, clung to the wreckage for ten days before giving in to sheer exhaustion.

Young James left home at fifteen and shipped before the mast on the schooner *Kittie,* which plied the waters of Huron and Erie with cargoes of lumber. In those days Michigan was the greatest producer of pine in the United States. At the age of sixteen, he became mate of the schooner *Hannah Moore* and the next year the youngest full master of a sailing vessel on the Great Lakes.

The youthful skipper saw that steam was soon going to supersede sail completely on the Lakes. So he gave up his command and entered the new field as a wheelsman on the steamer *Averill* and later on the *Haskell.* His step to the quarterdeck came as mate of the *Cambria,* the first steel steamer built by Mark Hanna. In 1890 he was appointed master of his first steamer, the *Havana,* also a Hanna vessel.

At the time of the Great Storm, Captain Watts had sailed the Lakes for a period of thirty-three years and had been a master of steamships for twenty-three. He knew the Lakes so well he was drafted into the Lighthouse Service and was master of the U. S. tender *Warrington.* As such, he was responsible for the placing of all the range lights in the Soo River. He knew where they were needed, for he'd been the first master to navigate the Soo after dark. He knew the dangers of the Lakes, too, for he'd been ship-wrecked twice in the old sailing days.

This, then, was the man who faced the Storm in all its fury, giving back as good as he got. And this is his story:

"The steamer *J. F. Durston* passed Lake Huron Lightship at the foot of the lake at about 9:00 P.M. Saturday, November 8. We were bound for Milwaukee with a cargo of soft coal. The wind was northwest fresh.

"About 2:30 A.M. Sunday, we were off Harbor Beach, which is about sixty miles farther north. The wind was north-northwest and quite a sea was running. By 9:30 or 10:00 A.M., it was blowing a gale from due north, with a big sea running. The engineer, Edward Sampson, was throttling the engine because of its racing. We soon had a lively time of it. By noon it was blowing a hurricane from the same quarter. Ice was forming and the blinding snow had started.

"Just before she settled down to some real blowing, we passed the steamer *Hydrus* and exchanged passing signals. They were the last she ever blew, for she went down with her entire crew a few hours later.

"By 1:30 Sunday afternoon, we were off Thunder Bay Isle, which is about 150 miles from Port Huron. We were under check and not making much headway. The sea was too heavy for me to try to make a lee at Thunder Bay, so I kept the *Durston* heading into it, steering north. The sea was increasing all the time and our decks and hatches were coating up with huge masses of ice."

Captain Watts here had to make the hardest decision of his trip. He wasn't going to be panicked into trying for that lee. He wasn't going to be tricked into the deadly trough of the sea. As nearly as we can guess, other men did try for other havens but they didn't live to tell of their last dangerous grasp for safety. Captain Watts pushed on.

"About 5:00 P.M. Sunday, the storm doors throughout the ship washed away and the shutters on the windows started to cave in. It was snowing heavy and freezing hard. I had the engineer check the propeller down to fifty-five turns a minute. By 6:00 P.M., it wasn't safe for a man to try to get from for'd aft or from aft for'd. The lifeline was covered with solid ice, which made it as thick around as a man's body and absolutely useless.

"The sea was coming over us from both sides. It was terrible

—higher than the cabins, it would swoop down and break over
the top of the after cabins with a thunderous crash. Never in all
my years on the Lakes do I remember such terrible seas. No man
could have lived in them. All the lifeboats, life rafts and life belts
in the world wouldn't have been worth a tinker's damn. In that
black seething water these so-called 'safety-aids' couldn't have
lasted a minute.

"At any time from 6:00 P.M. until after midnight, we would
have met our end had the *Durston* got into the trough of those
waves. They would have ripped our hatches off, filled us, and
sent us to the bottom in less time than it takes to explain. Fortunately, we didn't have much trouble keeping head on to the sea.
Checking her down was the answer. It gave the ship a chance to
rise with the sea, for lake steamers, when loaded deeper than two-
thirds of the molded depth, are loggy and lift with difficulty.

"The one mercy the storm showed us was to seal our hatches
and for'd cabins and windows with a thick armor-plating of ice.
Fortunately, too, our bunker was filled with coal to above the
spar deck, which helped to strengthen the cabins against the
seas. Rising to the waves massing higher and higher before her,
the *Durston* pushed on steadily through the heart of the Storm.
The wind blew hardest from 8:00 P.M. Sunday until midnight.

"We made virtually no time at all while the fury was at its
height. We just kept bucking steadily into the seas which swept
us from every quarter. The course was due north. At midnight
the wind started to die down a little, although of course it was
with us all night, blowing from north to northeast.

"From 1:30 Sunday afternoon, when we were abreast of Thunder Bay Isle, until 9:00 Monday morning, when we drew abreast
of Spectacle Reef, a distance of sixty miles, we never knew exactly
where we were. The last time we worried about it much was at
8:00 Sunday night. We figured we were off between Middle Isle
and False Presque Isle. They can talk all they want about sounding machines and patent logs, but ours didn't do us a bit of good.
They were both out of commission because of the ice.

"We sighted Spectacle Reef about 8:00 A.M. Monday. We
were steering west and the wind was northwest and strong, but
not as bad as on Sunday. We came to anchor at Mackinaw about
1:00 P.M., Monday. It had taken forty hours for the run from

Lake Huron Lightship to Mackinaw, normally a run of less than twenty-two hours.

"The *Durston* looked like a ghost ship. She was covered by about a thousand tons of ice. All around her pilot house and cabins and over the entire deck the ice was at least a foot thick."

Captain Watts doesn't tell this one himself but it's still told on him by others. When Watts docked his ship at Mackinaw after his encounter with the Storm, some bold person in the welcoming crowd ventured to suggest that the skipper might have been, perhaps—well, just a little—worried during the hurricane.

"Hell! No!" roared the skipper. "I'm a sailor! I don't start worryin' until my ship starts leaking and I can't find the leak!"

But as Ed Sampson, the chief engineer of the *Durston* said, "Only a skipper kissed by Lady Luck could have come through that storm! I could feel his anxiety all the time, especially after the first wave smashed into the pilot house."

After his first outburst, Captain Watts went on a bit more quietly. "Well, all I had to do was to keep her heading into it and out of the trough. It's mighty lucky our steering gear held up under the terrific pressure. I always make it a point to inspect it personally."

It took a man like that, a bold sailor who "always inspected it personally," to do what Captain Watts did. That combination of courage and common sense beat the storm.

"Ship's all right, it's the men in her," said Watts, "for a ship is no better than the men who take her out."

CHAPTER 5

The Saga of the Waldo

OF ALL THE ships that met disaster in the Great Storm, the *L. C. Waldo* met it most quickly. While many other ships gave in only after fighting for hours, the *Waldo* had two strikes called on her immediately after the Storm struck Lake Superior. The tale of the *Waldo* is one of incredible survival against overwhelming odds and of a heroic rescue—a story of devotion to duty in the great tradition of the sea.

The direct cause of the *Waldo*'s destruction was the almost fatal loss of her steering wheel and pilot house, which were swept away by the mighty seas in the very beginning of the blow. She was bound from Two Harbors to Cleveland with a full cargo of iron ore. Without any warning she was struck by the Storm seventy-six miles west of Keweenaw Point early Saturday morning.

Captain Duddleson and Louis Feeger, second mate, were in

the pilot house when the mountainous seas began to batter the vessel as she headed for shelter at Slate Island on the north shore of Lake Superior. The pilot house windows were caked with a solid mass of ice and the skipper was steering entirely by compass, the angry seas in massed attack behind him.

It was only a few minutes after the Storm struck that the seas roared down on the freighter, tossing it skywards, first stern, then bow. Then the waters tore across the deck and swept on. It seemed to the men on board as if the wind would blow the ship right out of the water.

Suddenly a towering sea, more mountainous than any of the previous ones, howled up astern. The captain couldn't see the giant sea heading toward him but he could plainly hear the crest above the other thunderous noises.

"By God, stand by for a big one. Here it comes!" he shouted into the telephone. Every man braced his feet, held on to whatever was at hand, and waited for the shock.

The ship lifted. But not quickly enough. With a tremendous crash, the crest broke directly overhead and thundered down over the ship's entire superstructure. The pilot house and cabins went over the side like so much kindling wood; the compass and binnacle followed them. Everything went but the auxiliary steering gear. Even the lighting equipment was destroyed.

As the pilot house crumbled away into the howling darkness, captain and mate leaped for their lives into the hatchway below. They were dragged under the seething foam by what seemed to be the suction of the ship's sinking. The force of the water was so great that they were pinned against the bottom of the foremast as if nailed there. They could think of no explanation but that the ship had disintegrated and was going down.

They had barely managed to draw breath before they were pulled under again by another giant sea. Again they kept on sinking. Gasping for air and soaked to the skin by the icy water, they instinctively grasped at whatever they found within reach as the sea lifted them again and again from their feet. Miraculously, they were not knocked unconscious.

Fighting their way in the blackness, they crawled painfully

across the slippery deck on all fours trying their best to keep from swimming themselves into the open water. Finally they reached the forward deck house but here the sleet and snow only multiplied their troubles.

Captain Duddleson was calm and resourceful. He talked little and thought much. He and the mate were two silent heroic men carrying on their responsible jobs. With the pilot house and compass gone, and all the lights with them, they steered the course by means of a small auxiliary wheel and a tiny compass such as every Boy Scout has in his possession. The mate held the compass on a broken stool, watching the dial by the flickering rays of a hand lantern.

Navigating a long bulk freighter in a gale is a nerve-wracking experience at best, but in such a situation as Captain Duddleson's it was deadly. Every nerve was taut as he listened to the thundering noises outside the ship. He used every bit of his skill and knowledge to keep afloat.

From his position in the battered deck house, his tired eyes on the tiny compass, he could hear the brutal destruction taking place aft. Every side roll of the vessel was followed by a pitch forward into the raging seas. Then another wave would lift the bow to start the side roll again.

Several times he lifted his eyes from the little compass and peered back as a wave bigger than usual roared over the stern. What he saw made him doubt the ship would live to see another sunrise. The ship's deck was completely blotted out by a solid wall of water. The sight was enough to make the strongest man pale. The deafening thunder of wind and sea was mingled with the noise of the destruction of the superstructures.

Since no calculation of position could be made in the absence of lights and instruments, even if the pilot house had been intact, Captain Duddleson had little idea of his location.

Suddenly he heard the surf beating on Gull Rock and Manitou Island. To his horror, the ship was bearing directly toward the massive rocks. His face, haggard with fatigue and anxiety, blanched a trifle more. Mate and captain looked incredulously at each other.

"My God, Mr. Feeger. We're gonners," gasped the captain.

The tragic note in his voice clearly indicated that there was nothing further he or the crew could possibly do that would stave off the death they sensed a moment ahead.

Driven by the ninety-mile hurricane the ship struck the rocks, and broke in two immediately.

At the terrible mercy of wind and sea, it wasn't long before everything went over the sides—forward deckhouse, where the captain and mate had fought with their tiny compass, cabins, mast, stack, life rafts, lifeboats—everything smashed to flotsam. The *Waldo* was a pitiful sight.

The crew's plight seemed hopeless. The twenty-seven men and two women were numb with fear, honestly expecting to be buried beneath the waves before help arrived. Only the bravery of Rice, the steward, of Johnson, a fireman, and of Charles Keefer, an engineer, saved the lives of the women, Mrs. Rice, wife of the steward, and Mrs. Mackie, her mother.

The women were huddled in the dining room aft when the *Waldo* went on the rocks. The noise of the wind and surf and destruction drove the women into hysterics. It was hardly necessary for the mate to shout the warning to the crew aft, "All hands for'd! Tumble out quick!" for most of this was drowned out by the tumult. At any rate, the crew instinctively rushed forward to seek safety in the forepeak. That is, all but the women. They were too paralyzed with fear to move or make the smallest effort to help themselves.

Rice and Johnson, who were almost the last to leave the stern, grabbed Mrs. Rice and dragged her across the four hundred feet of treacherous ice-covered deck, forward to safety. Several times the men with their half-conscious battling burden, were swept from their feet by the seas which continually came aboard. Their lives were saved only because they never released their grip on the steel cable railing.

Keefer, the last man left in the stern of the wreck, started across the deck with Mrs. Mackie. When the first smashing wave hit them, Mrs. Mackie fought like a mad animal to get free. She wanted to return to the dining room, which was fast breaking apart. Keefer, however, held her tight around the waist and struck her feet from under her in order to carry her better. Mercifully for both of them, she then lost consciousness. Keefer struggled across the deck with the unconscious woman in his arms. He said afterward that "the terrible trip across that icy waste seemed like a battle for hours with ice, wave and wind."

When they were opposite number two hatch in the forward end of the boat, a great sea struck them, pinning them both to the railing and driving the breath from Keefer's body. Other members of the crew rushed to his assistance. Another mighty wave tore Mrs. Mackie right out of his hands and carried her over the life rail. Everyone thought she was gone with the sea. But Keefer had retained a superhuman grip on her clothing and she was pulled in before the next wave could sweep her away.

When the *Waldo* broke in two, all access to her after part was cut off by the raging seas. Here were stored all the crew's provisions and clothing. With their clothes thoroughly soaked and quickly freezing to their bodies, they made desperate attempts to start a fire—no small job in their situation. They finally managed to build a small fire in a bathtub brought forward from the cabin. To this makeshift stove they attached a crude chimney made of water buckets with their bottoms knocked out. To keep the life-saving fires burning, the crew was forced to tear up everything that was combustible.

The only food available was one can of tomatoes and two cans of peaches. This was all the entire crew tasted during their ninety-hour imprisonment in the forepeak. The rest was washed overboard with the galley, and they would have been unable to reach the galley even if there had been food there.

On Sunday morning the steamer *George Stephenson* sighted them but could not reach them. She was on her way to rescue the *Waldo* as she disappeared in the storm, but the crew of the *Waldo* could have no way of knowing it. Captain Mosher had sailed away from a safe anchorage in Keweenaw Bay to bring them aid.

"At 5:00 P.M., Saturday," said Captain Mosher, "it stopped snowing and I saw we were about one mile sou'west of Keweenaw Point." He had had his own troubles in reaching that anchorage.

"On Sunday morning at daylight, I saw a steamer ashore at the northeast point of Manitou Island. She seemed to be abandoned; there were no lights on her and no smoke was coming from her stack. Her decks were out of water and the big seas were breaking over her. I knew there must be men aboard her but I wasn't sure. We first knew definitely when we saw a distress signal go up on her foremast at 7:00 A.M.

"After hoisting a flag in answer, we hove up and went to Mendota on the tip of Keweenaw Peninsula. There I sent the mate ashore to find a telephone and notify the lifesavers. By hiring a motorboat from a fisherman to get across Lac La Belle and a horse and sleigh to reach Delaware, he succeeded in sending a message to the Eagle Harbor Lifesaving Station."

When news of the *Waldo's* plight reached the station, an immediate attempt at rescue was made. Fortunately, the lifesavers were not dependent on oars and sails alone. About ten years back, the federal government had introduced power boats to help in the rescue and salvage work of the Lifesaving Service. As was usual, there were two boats at the Eagle Harbor Station, one an eight horsepower surfboat, the other larger and more powerful. Unfortunately, the more powerful boat was undergoing repairs.

Although the distance to the scene of the wreck was thirty-two miles and the state of the weather obviously perilous to the smaller boat, the Eagle Harbor crew hastened to get under way. But after only eight miles out in the open seas and exposed to the full force of the Storm, the boat became so encrusted with ice that it was unmanageable. The crew, drenched by the icy water, were fast succumbing to chill and frostbite. Realizing that in a short time they would be helpless themselves, Keeper Charles A. Tucker reluctantly gave his orders, "It's no use, boys. Turn back."

The eight mile return to the station was almost fatal to the rescuing crew. The surfmen were so coated with ice when they reached their station that they had to call on others to release them from their life belts and outer garments. Without rest, however, the surfmen set to work to get the larger lifeboat in condition for duty.

Meanwhile, Captain Mosher of the *Stephenson* was chafing under his forced inactivity.

"It blew hard and snowed Sunday night. I still felt uneasy about the men on the stranded steamer. Next morning I sent the second mate ashore with orders to get definite news and, if the men hadn't been rescued, to call up the Portage Lake Ship-Canal Lifesaving Station near Hancock.

"The mate learned that Eagle Harbor had made an attempt but had been forced to turn back. When he called the Portage Station he was told they had not been notified but would start work immediately by taking their boat by railroad flatcar to Lac La Belle. The lifesavers would make the run to the wreck from there. He called again at 2:00 P.M., and found they had started a half-hour before. We had a fierce blizzard from then until 5:00 P.M."

The shortest distance by boat from Portage Lake Station to Gull Rock is about sixty miles but a boat taking this route would be exposed to the gale the entire distance. A more indirect route was open through the ship canal to Portage Entry on the southerly shore of Keweenaw Point and from there across the open lake. This was a journey of eighty miles, but the lifesavers would be under the lee of the peninsula most of the way and so somewhat protected from the Storm.

With this in mind, the keeper of the station, Thomas H. Mc-Cormick, decided upon the longer route. Before starting out, he sent a message asking the tug *Daniel L. Hebard* to meet him as he came from the canal and take him in tow.

In the meantime, while the Eagle Harbor and Portage crews were trying to reach them, the victims on the *Waldo* were enduring long hours of suffering. There was nothing they could do to better their position. After the rescue of the women from the after part of the wreck, Keefer and Johnson had returned below to Engineer Lemke in the engine room. While Johnson kept firing the boiler, Lemke and Keefer kept the engine working for an hour in a vain attempt to drive the vessel further ashore. When they gave up and returned above deck, Keefer saw the complete hopelessness of their position.

"We never expected to reach shore alive," he said. "As far as we could see the shore was lined with rocks twenty to forty feet high. We had one lifeboat that we might possibly have used, but it would have been suicide to attempt a landing."

Huddled together in the forepeak around the bathtub with its small wood fire, without food or blankets, the crew was desperate. There was nothing to say, nothing to do, and all of them had long ago thought all there was to think. Members of the crew who couldn't find room in the forepeak were forced to lash themselves to stanchions and other fixed parts of the ship to keep from being washed overboard. They all expected within the next five, ten, or perhaps fifteen minutes, to be battered to death by the huge waves. Then the snow, which had stopped when the *Stephenson* sighted them on Sunday, began to fall again.

"We had a fierce blizzard all day Monday until 5:00 P.M.," said Captain Mosher. "Then it stopped snowing and the wind eased up a bit. I hove up at 9:20 P.M., came through Gull Rock and saw the *Waldo* still with her decks above water. She was lying lifeless and silent in the night."

Even while the captain of the *Stephenson* was looking at her, the Portage lifesaving crew were nearing the end of their fourteen hour run to the scene. The seas were continually breaking over their lifeboat, completely burying her at times. Their boat was a self-bailer, but her outlet valve froze up and her men had to chop the constantly forming ice from the valve openings. She was very hard to handle, the mass of ice on decks and bulkheads causing her to list dangerously.

But in spite of all their difficulties, the Portage crew arrived at the scene in tow of the tug *Hebard* at 3:00 A.M. Tuesday.

As they took shelter under Keweenaw Point to wait for daylight, the Eagle Harbor crew, having finished the necessary repairs to the larger boat, with the forty horsepower engine, were starting for the wreck for the second time.

After the *Stephenson* left the scene, apparently leaving the *Waldo* crew to their fate, that tortured company caught no further sight of a ship, and despaired of help coming in time. All they saw were mountainous icy-green seas and destruction going on around them. Imagine their excitement when, from their precarious shelter, they suddenly sighted an ice-encrusted lifeboat topping a wave, then sinking out of sight, and at last reappearing through the haze.

There were no hosannas or shouts of greeting, only a surge of activity, a mad desire to do something after the days and nights of hopeless inaction. Thank God there was something they could do about it now!

"A-h-o-y." The first hail the Portage crew heard was a shout to stand by until the *Waldo* crew could chop their way through the ice which imprisoned them in their shelter.

In the meantime, the lifesavers from Eagle Harbor arrived on the scene. Together, the two lifesaving crews worked in toward the wreck.

Because of the position in which she lay, the *Waldo* offered very little lee to the two surfboats, no matter from which quarter they approached her. The wreck was hemmed in by the huge ice-covered rocks. Nevertheless, the two boats moved in slowly, cautiously yet bravely, as soon as the *Waldo* crew were in a position to help themselves. As they lay alongside the *Waldo,* the surfboats rose with each swell, then slid into the trough beneath a rush of water from above. In spite of the hazards and handicaps, they kept beside the *Waldo* and members of the lifesaving crew even managed to board the *Waldo* and assist in taking off the exhausted and sick seamen.

The lethargy of extreme fatigue was upon the *Waldo* crewmen. They were in a pitiful condition indeed. Their bones and muscles ached, their eyes were bloodshot from lack of sleep, and their pain-wracked faces gave evidence of the physical and spiritual struggle they had experienced.

Fast work was essential. Every minute was perilous to both rescuer and rescued, and many of the latter were nearing the extreme point of exhaustion.

"Part of the *Waldo*'s crew was taken on board by means of a rope ladder," said McCormick of the Portage crew. "Others leaped from her deck."

Each time one of the boats rose on a swell, one of those still able to help himself would leap, to be caught in the arms of the lifesavers. A sure leap it had to be, for if a man had fallen into the water he would have been lost. The lifeboats, therefore, had to be kept grimly, dangerously close to the steel hull.

"Ten men were loaded into our boat without serious accident," said McCormick. "The rest, including the two women, were taken into the boat from Eagle Harbor."

The women were thrown into the lifeboats since they could not, or were afraid to, jump. No one could blame them. One glance at the seething surf and it took a mighty strong man to keep his nerve.

With the *Waldo* crew in the comparative safety of the surf-boats, the wreck was utterly abandoned, left to break up by herself on towering Gull Rock. Slowly and carefully the two lifeboats drew away from her side through the treacherous surf.

It was still a long dangerous stretch to the waiting tug. On came the waves, raising the bows almost perpendicularly. When it seemed that the sea would surely break over the stern and fill the boat, the seamen would find instead that they were cleared, and next the bow would settle while the stern rose—so high they expected to be thrown into the surf.

The crew of the *Waldo* had no heavy clothing and what clothing they had on was soaked and clinging to their bodies in icy folds.

"They were all in and nearly frozen," said surfman A. F. Glaza of the Eagle Harbor crew. "Some had towels wrapped around their heads and some were wearing socks for mittens. Most of them had neither. We put our mackinaws and caps on them until we managed to get them to the tug. The women cried for joy when we wrapped them in warm blankets. When we put them on the tug they immediately offered up a prayer of thanksgiving and asked the blessing of Heaven upon our captain and his crew."

"The tug had come provided with 100 pounds of ham and a crate of eggs," said Keefer of the *Waldo*. "But, gee, we were so weak it was agony to eat. Some of the men, however, crammed the food into their mouths like cannibals. We hadn't eaten for more than ninety hours."

Well the *Waldo* crew might have offered a prayer of thanksgiving for their miraculous deliverance. They had been driven for many hours, blind and helpless, before a savage gale. They had fetched up on a deadly shore with the full force of that gale behind them. Their ship had broken in two on those rocks, yet she had clung to them long enough to permit their rescue. One of their rescuers had reached them only on the second attempt.

The other had fought the storm for fourteen solid hours to reach them.

And not one life was lost.

From the warm shelter and comfort of the tug they could look back to where the *Waldo* lay broken and doomed, still hammered by the relentless seas.

"Thank God we're alive," said Captain Duddleson. "It's the closest call I ever had in all my life."

Hanging on the walls of the Lifesaving Stations at Eagle Harbor and Portage Lake are two famous letters, matted and framed and placed where they catch the eye as one enters the main rooms. They will always be reminders of the Great Storm. They read as follows:

> There is transmitted herewith a gold medal of honor, awarded to you by this Department under Acts of Congress, May 4, 1882, in recognition of your heroic conduct upon the occasion of the rescue of the steamer *L. C. Waldo*, which went ashore on Manitou Island, Lake Superior, during the Great Storm of November 8–11, 1913.
>
> It affords the Department great pleasure to have this opportunity to commend the services rendered by you at that time.
>
> > Respectfully
> > Byron R. Newton
> > Assistant Secretary
> > Treasury Department

CHAPTER 6

Abandoned

THE MOST complete account we have of any
wreck during the Storm of 1913 is that of the steamer *Howard M.
Hanna, Jr.* It is unusual in one important respect: in addition to
the narrative of Captain Hagen we have the story of the ship's
experiences told from a below-decks viewpoint by Chief Engineer
Mayberry.

"I was the last master of the fine steamer *Howard M. Hanna,
Jr.,*" related Captain Hagen. "I had been master of Lakes vessels
for about twenty-five years and had been in the employ of Captain
Richardson's fleet for twelve years as master of different vessels.

"On this last trip we left Lorain, Ohio, bound for Fort William,
Ontario, on Saturday, November 8, at 10:00 A.M. We were loaded
with 9200 tons of soft coal, and had a full complement of officers
and crew—twenty-five men including myself. We had taken on
fuel at Lorain and had about 325 tons of coal for our bunker. We

therefore had plenty to make the round trip and also provisions enough to last at least the twenty-day round trip, as we didn't want to pick up supplies at Fort William.

"When we left Lorain, the vessel was in ideal trim for encountering heavy weather. The cargo had been loaded so that it was flush with the hatch coamings, and there was no chance of its shifting. The hatches had been battened down and we had tarpaulins with hatch bars and windy youngs. The bars were placed three athwartship on each hatch and there were three windy youngs fore-and-aft on each hatch. Everything was secured, everything movable had proper lashings and the vessel was as staunch and seaworthy as possible.

"When we got out into Lake Huron the weather was good. The wind was west of north, maybe a fifteen-mile breeze off the land. We passed Fort Gratiot Lightship at 5:12 A.M. Sunday. The weather continued fair and clear until after we passed Harbor Beach; but the wind had shifted, first southeast for a few minutes, then northeast, and finally north-northeast. It continued from about that direction with increasing velocity.

"We passed Harbor Beach at 11:30 A.M., with the wind increasing rapidly from the same direction. Up until 3:00 P.M., there were only slight snow flurries, nothing unusual, but at that time it began to snow heavily. As the wind had increased considerably, we hauled more to the northward to hold her head to the wind. We passed Pointe Aux Barques near Port Austin about 2:00 P.M., nearly five miles off the Pointe."

About this time, Engineer Mayberry went down into the engine room to take personal charge. Until then matters had not been too serious. The vessel had been making only small headway with her engines at full speed, but the extra supply of fuel coal could have stood such a drain for a considerable period.

"With every bit of the ship's power," said Mayberry, "we had to face tremendous waves. Immediately I started the syphons and pumps going to keep the ever increasing floods of water out. I put up canvases over the dynamo to make sure that nothing would stop the action of the pumps. Everything went reasonably well. It wasn't until four hours later that the trouble really started.

"About 6:30 P.M., the bloody destruction began. The oiler's door on the starboard side was the first to get smashed in, and shortly afterward the two engine room doors and windows went. It was terrible. Tons of icy water were pouring into the engine room. The whole place was a damn mess. We stood knee deep in the swirling ice water and more kept rushing in.

"Throughout this confusion I kept in contact with the captain by telephone. He frequently called to ask if the engine was working all right and I informed him it was. We mustn't yield to the weather, he said. We needed all the power we could possibly get to keep the ship headed into the wind.

"The next bloody break came when the windows and doors of the engineer's room went in at 7:30. That must have opened the breach, for after that it seemed as if everything else went in order. The cook's room and dining room went. The woodwork was carried away, part coming into the engine room to add to the wreckage already piling up there, and part going overboard."

Above deck too, conditions were going from bad to worse. "Tremendous seas were coming over our bow and starboard quarters," said Captain Hagen, "over the whole vessel in fact. They carried away part of the after cabin, broke in the windows and doors of the pilot house and tore off its top. Although the engines were working at full speed ahead, the vessel began dropping off her course, and there was nothing we could do about it.

"Between 7:00 and 8:00 P.M., it was snowing so hard we couldn't see land. It was impossible to judge our exact position or gauge our speed, but we must have been about fifteen miles off Pointe Aux Barques.

"Then shortly afterward, the ship dropped off so that she came around into the trough of the sea, which we had tried so desperately to avoid. We had been taking seas over us right along and we had been using our syphons and pumps, but we knew she was taking in water by the way the pumps worked.

"After she got into the trough she commenced to roll and tumble, and the mountainous seas smashed over her. The propeller wheel was out of water and it was impossible for us to bring the ship back to head into the sea, or to keep her off before the sea. In spite of our every effort, we lay in the trough, rolling heavily, with the seas washing over us."

" 'Can't we do anything?' cried the crew when she hove her decks free of the overwhelming torrents for a moment. I don't know of anything more we could have done," said Mayberry. "All the engine room crew did their best, even when water was coming in in torrents.

"The captain telephoned regularly to keep in touch with our condition, and told me with a slow, awed voice of the unsuccessful fight going on forward to bring her head into it. He seemed particularly anxious about the steering gear. Since the chains pass through the engine room, I could see and hear them working all right. I knew our plight was not due to engine or steering gear failure—the Storm was just too much for us."

Meanwhile a new danger, unseen by the engine room crew, was threatening the ship. "Shortly before 10:00 P.M.," said Captain Hagen, "we could see the Port Austin light as we lay rolling in the seas. The bearing of the light was nearly southwest off our port bow and we saw that we were dangerously close to Port Austin reef.

"I ordered the first mate to drop our anchors. He went down into the windlass room and let go the port anchor in order to bring her head to the wind. She came around only about a point and to our dismay continued drifting steadily toward her doom.

"In a very short time the great waves rode her to destruction. She drifted broadside into the reef at 10:00 P.M. The port side fetched up on the rocks first and the seas and wind pounded her the rest of the way onto the reef. She listed badly to starboard and filled with water right up to the deck, and the hatches were all washed off."

"She sure was a broken-down steamer rolling in that snow storm," said Mayberry. "The smoke stack bent over and was carried away about the time we struck. Throughout the entire struggle before we went on the rocks, the engines and all the machinery of the ship were working perfectly and we still had 250 tons of fuel coal left. We fetched up on the reef about six hundred feet northeast of Port Austin light, heading northeast by north."

"As she struck, the forward crew all came up into the texas to get shelter," continued Captain Hagen, "and remained there until the weather had moderated on Monday afternoon. The after crew remained aft in the messroom and kitchen. We had no means of communication with each other. On Monday the third engineer worked his way forward with food. We all managed to get together in the kitchen sometime Tuesday morning.

"As we scrambled aft we noticed that the vessel was broken in two about the after side of number seven hatch. You could see the wide crack across the deck and down the side. The smoke stack was gone, and the life rafts and starboard lifeboat had been carried away. She had a terrific starboard list. Her bows were about ten feet lower than her stern. Half the fuel hatch and the boiler house had been washed overboard. The starboard side and the after end of the cabin had also been carried away, leaving just the kitchen and the mess room and the hard coal box. The houses forward were all stove in, the doors and windows knocked out, the top of the pilot house gone, and the bulwarks forward driven in. The vessel was a total loss."

Engineer Mayberry said that when the break was first noticed it was about three inches wide, but by the time the crew left the vessel it had increased to eight inches.

With the ship breaking up around them, the crew wondered at the prospects of rescue. Actually their distress signal had been sighted through a rift in the blizzard at about 8:30 A.M., Monday. The same Storm which had wrecked them, however, held up their rescue.

Like many other Lake Huron lifesaving crews, the Port Austin men had to meet seemingly insurmountable difficulties before they could go out. Their boathouse and dock had been wrecked and their surfboat buried in the sand by the storm. They put their small lifeboat on a wagon, carried it down to the shore, and launched it about a mile north of the station. The crew fought through the heavy seas out as far as Gull Rock, a full half mile from shore. Here the lifeboat filled and the men were compelled to turn back, reaching shore again only with great difficulty.

Surfman Deegan was sent to Port Austin to telephone the neighboring lifesaving stations at Harbor Beach and Huron City for help. Both stations were busy on wrecks of their own, the Harbor Beach Station having four vessels in trouble.

So the Port Austin crew were forced to try digging out their surfboat from the mountain of drifted sand. Being equipped with a centerboard, it was more seaworthy than the smaller boat. When they got the heavier boat free, they found her gunwale broken in five places, a large hole in her after platform, and numerous holes in her bottom. It was late that night before they finished patching her up.

On Tuesday morning they started out once more. As they made their hazardous way to the wreck, they met some of the *Hanna's* crew coming toward shore in the ship's boat. At daylight that morning, the mate of the *Hanna* had gone up on the after cabin with some of the crew and cleared the ice and water out of the port lifeboat, the only one that had not been carried away. At 7:30 A.M., they lowered the lifeboat and nine of the crew started for shore to get help for the rest. It was 10:00 A.M. when the two boats passed each other on their respective errands of mercy.

The lifesavers took six men and a woman off the *Hanna* on their first trip. The steward's wife was wearing men's clothes and was so overcome by exposure that it was feared she would die before they reached the station. She had floundered about in the galley in ice water waist deep, trying to prepare a much needed meal for the crew.

The patched surfboat leaked so badly on the return trip to shore, with the extra weight, that the lifesavers had to head straight for the beach to keep from sinking. Landing their first group of shivering and blueskinned shipwreck victims, they bailed out the boat and hastily returned to the *Hanna*.

As they lay alongside the ship, their boat filled again. They bailed her out once more, took aboard the remainder of the crew, and made a bee-line for shore. Hoisting a sail this time, they made sufficient speed to complete the rescue safely.

The survivors and lifesavers were welcomed on the shore by townspeople who had heard of the rescue. The welcome was of the right kind, for it included pails of hot coffee. The rescued were then taken to much needed shelter and a dinner at a local hotel.

The lifesavers returned to their station, with their boat on a sleigh. The survivors went their individual ways to rest and recuperate. And out on the reef lay the *Hanna*, abandoned. She had been insured for $315,000.

CHAPTER 7

Taking the Ground

"Taking the ground" was not a pleasant thing in the Great Storm. There is no sound the sailor hates more than the grinding of his vessel's hull on the bottom, and no feeling worse than that of her once-floating body stopping dead as the rocks or the sand holds her fast. And there is no danger greater than that of being pounded to pieces on a lee shore. This chapter is concerned with ships that took the ground in the Great Storm.

The *William Nottingham,* grain laden, down bound from Port Arthur, Ontario, went aground in the heavy gale Monday morning on a reef between Sand Island and Parisian Island at the western end of Lake Superior. Her position was a perilous one. She had struck hard and the pounding of the waves soon buckled her in the center. The fight with the wind and seas on the way down the lake had been so strenuous that the supply of coal in her bunkers was exhausted. The wheat that composed her cargo was used to keep up the fires under her boilers and give heat to the exhausted crew.

In this plight, it is little wonder that an attempt to reach shore, however foolhardy, was made. A vessel afloat takes a bad enough beating from big seas, but one held hard and fast on the rocks is as helpless against the breakers as a man trussed up to a whipping post. It is hard even for brave men to sit still and take it. In a desperate attempt to bring help for their vessel, a wheelsman, an oiler, and a deckhand were lowered over the side in the ship's lifeboat. The small boat had no sooner reached the water than it was overturned by the oncoming sea, hurling the three men into the icy water. Their shipmates on the spar deck tried frantically to reach them, but all their attempts were futile. Weighted down with heavy clothing and numbed by the freezing cold, the three quickly disappeared beneath the waves. Even if they had been equipped for swimming, and the temperature of the water had been less chilling, they could not have survived longer than a few seconds, for the human body is not built to fight and conquer hurricane seas that can break and swamp huge steel freighters. The tragedy was over in a moment.

The rest of the crew was finally rescued by the lifesavers, and the *Nottingham* lay on the reef until quiet weather, when wreckers arrived. After several weeks of hard work they succeeded in releasing her and taking her to Toledo for repairs which amounted to $75,000. Her grain cargo, insured for $200,000, was a total loss.

It is a great tribute to the Lifesaving Service that not a single life was lost on those vessels in distress that it was notified of and was able to reach. Whatever the condition of its tiny boats, the Service had the skill to use them in rough waters. That other crews lacked this skill is evidenced by what occurred at the wreck of the *Nottingham*.

Another ship that took the ground during the Great Storm was the steamer *J. T. Hutchinson*. H. J. Yacques of the *Hutchinson* wrote to his wife while the vessel was stranded on Point Iroquois in Whitefish Bay. His letter, which was reproduced in the Detroit *News* a few days after the Storm, reveals some of the strain he must have been under, although he naturally tried to minimize it for his wife's sake:

I suppose that you will read about the loss of the *J. T. Hutchinson*, but don't worry, for I think that we will be all right if she doesn't go to pieces or break in two. We are on the rocks and cold.

I am in the pilot house at present, and all we can do is to wait for the wind to go down, so some relief can come to us. If it were not for the heavy sea that is running, our decks would be clear of water, but they are awash all the time and the ice is terrible. I will give you an outline of what this trip has been from Duluth.

We were 30 hours loading. Rain and snow all the time and ore frozen solid. We left the dock at Duluth at 3:45 A.M., Saturday, November 8th. We were not well outside of the breakwall before she started to ship water. Then, as the wind was northeast, we started for the north shore, that is, the Canadian side of Lake Superior, steering northeast quarter east to clear Two Harbors, than hauled northeast by east, and then our troubles began.

We shipped water and expected to see our hatches go at any minute; no breakfast or dinner. Off watch at 12 noon and called at 2:30 to stand by. The coal bunker hatch had been torn away and we worked 16 hours.

All wet, clothes frozen and my rubber boots full of water and six hours' watch ahead of me. No change of weather, Ship log broke, lost all track of distance and don't know where we are.

6:30 A.M. Sunday—See mainland about ten miles north-ward of us but cannot tell where we are. Run all the way steering northeast three-eighths east. Sight Isle Royale at 9:30 Sunday night. Snowing so we cannot see the entrance, so we have to make the best of it and stay outside.

1:30 A.M. Monday—Sight Battle Isle, Canadian side, snow-ing. We cannot get to shelter. We finally get to shelter at Carribeau [Caribou] Isle, but the wind has shifted us, so we will try and move for Whitefish Point and we have a hard run all the way. Nobody can sleep and everybody wet and hungry.

11:45 Monday night—See Whitefish Point light and make entrance all o.k. and everybody is happy. Little we thought that in less than five hours we would be on the rocks and have the ship going to pieces under us.

There are 23 of a crew here and we are all mighty tired

and miserably hungry but we have all done our best and we
have not any thought of losing out, within half a mile of good
dry land. We can't launch any of our lifeboats—too much
sea running. I don't know what will be done next but will
write any chance I get. The tug is here and I can send this
now.

The *Hutchinson* did not break up as Yacques feared, but was
later released and towed to Lorain, Ohio, for repairs which cost
above $40,000.

The Lifesaving Service was not called to the assistance of the
Hutchinson, or of the *F. G. Hartwell,* which struck ground in her
immediate vicinity. The revenue cutter *Mackinac* was the first to
reach them.

"We found the *Hutchinson* and the *Hartwell* hard aground
near Point Iroquois," says Captain Wheeler of the *Mackinac.*
"The bottoms of both steamers were badly torn by the big boulders
which lay along the shores. The *Hutchinson* was above the Point
while the *Hartwell* lay below. The first thing the masters asked
was 'Have you anything to eat? We're all out.' The *Hartwell's*
crew was worn and tired. The big steamer lay on her side with a
heavy list to port."

The *Hartwell* had struck the rocks about a mile southeast of
Iroquois Light and had sunk immediately in twenty-six feet of
water. Her cargo hold was flooded but her forward compartments
and engine room were dry. The crew was thus able to keep up
steam and keep themselves warm in the after quarters, although
the waves broke over them with terrific force all day Monday.
The ship was later floated, after her cargo of ore had been
lightered.

The steamer *Northern Queen,* unlike the *Hutchinson* and the
Hartwell, received help from shore, although for a while she was
in such danger that her crew was reported drowned. She was one
of the vessels that anchored when she had fought the seas to her
limit. She passed Port Huron up bound at 9:00 A.M. Sunday, but
in the terrible seas forty miles farther on she lost her headway.
There was but one thing to do—turn around and head back toward Port Huron. She finally managed to turn without capsizing
and by Monday morning she was within a quarter-mile of the
Lake Huron Lightship, close enough to see the lights of Port

Huron and to see a steamer which the crew knew was on the beach. They could hear the fog signals of the lighthouse above the roar of the hurricane.

Captain Crawford decided it would be folly to try to enter the St. Clair River with no control over the direction of the vessel. He must turn the *Queen* again. This time she managed to push thirty miles up Lake Huron before she had to give up. Not knowing that the dangerous shore of Port Franks was only eight miles off, Crawford decided to try his luck with the anchors. He fared no better than many others—the anchors could not hold her and at 7:00 P.M. Sunday, she went on the rocks.

The *Queen* was so close to shore that townspeople could see the faces of her crew, but they were as little able to help as if the ship were in mid-ocean. There seemed small hope. The waves battered her continuously, gradually breaking the after part to pieces.

Fortunately, the storm had passed its peak and it wasn't long before the lifesavers were assured of success. Late that night it was possible to begin the rescue. Though the *Queen* was beaten and broken, the length of time she had fought it out on the open lake saved her crew.

The steamer *Turret Chief* went through her final agony absolutely alone. In the blizzard and gale of Saturday on Lake Superior nobody knew of her plight. She was a splendid steel ship, originally built for trade in the stormy Baltic Sea. The Storm struck her on Friday afternoon on western Lake Superior, 110 miles west-northwest of Whitefish Point. Being light, she at first drifted rapidly and soon became unmanageable before the force of the gale. Although the captain and crew believed her to be well up in the center of the lake, by 4:00 A.M. Saturday, she was driven high on the beach at the extreme point of Keweenaw, six miles east of Copper Harbor. As she lay on the rocks Saturday, she was rapidly pounded to pieces.

The situation of the seventeen crew members was desperate. They managed to leave her Saturday afternoon and so were saved from a watery death as the ship disintegrated; but they were still helpless before the lashing of the storm. Saturday night and all day Sunday they huddled together in a hut of driftwood hastily erected on the shore.

On Monday they started out on foot and wandered through the heavy Michigan pine woods until Tuesday morning. The first intimation that anybody had of their plight was on their arrival in Mandan. They staggered into the snow-bound town, half frozen and thoroughly exhausted, having been without food or shelter for more than fifty hours in the bitter cold and raging blizzard.

On and on go the tales of men and ships fighting for their lives. Captain A. C. May of the steamer *H. A. Hawgood* fought one of the losing battles.

"I could have put my boat on the beach and spared myself and the crew a lot of hardship," he says, "but I did my best to save her. I actually had to crawl the few feet from one side of the small pilot house to the other. By God, that wind blew fully seventy-five miles an hour.

"We were up bound, light, on Lake Huron. When it was impossible to go on, I tried to make the shelter of the St. Clair River, but that was hopeless. I put out the anchors and prayed she'd hold, but anchors are bound to drag in such a gale. It was snowing so hard I couldn't see the smokestack, but I knew where I was within a mile or so. She dragged steadily for eight miles before she fetched up about two miles above Point Edward, Sarnia, Ontario.

"We struck so hard I was almost thrown out of the pilot house. Although she was light, the seas broke over her and the crew was in constant danger of being swept overboard. But for the crash on the beach just in time, there would have been another missing ship."

There were other masters who found it safer to be stranded on the beach than to be on the lake or even tied to a wharf. Captain McLean of the barge *Dorcas Pendell* was very emphatic on this point. "We came in in tow of the *Wyoming* Saturday night after rounding to off Port Austin," he said. "Then we tied to the main pier at Harbor Beach. The next day the storm, blowing ninety miles an hour, poured mountains of water over the breakwater and forced our boat, with every other boat in the harbor, from the lines on the pier. The wind was so strong that our anchors refused to hold and we were at the mercy of the storm.

"It was 12:30 A.M. Monday when we struck the nearby beach. The weather didn't clear up enough for another day so that we could even tell where we were. Then we discovered that we were just outside the steamers *Rhoda Emily* and the *Buckley,* both of which had been forced away from the pier and driven hard up on the beach."

One piece of criminal stupidity resulted in wrecking a freighter which might otherwise have ridden out the Storm safely. When *Lightship 61,* Corsica Shoal, was driven from her moorings at the height of Sunday's storm, she fetched up two miles south and east of her regular station in Lake Huron. Although she was not in any danger and had not been wrecked, her keeper refused to accept the responsibility of returning her to her proper berth without orders from the Chicago headquarters. His chief concern was whether or not he would get back the twenty-five dollars necessary to pay for towing her back to her proper station. Unless all his brains had gone into polishing the lenses of his lights, it's difficult to see how anyone calling himself a man could have taken such a view of things when every aid to navigation was a mortal necessity and other men were risking their lives to aid those in distress. The results were tragic.

When the steamer *Matthew Andrews* came down Lake Huron Sunday afternoon, loaded with iron ore, she made good progress, although the heavy seas swept the ship from stem to stern. Some distance to the north of the lifesaving station, Captain Lempoh saw he couldn't make the St. Clair River and decided to anchor and ride it out.

Unfortunately, he took his bearings for anchorage from the displaced lightship and drove straight to destruction instead of safety. Because of that incredible lightshipkeeper, who had forgotten every rule and tradition of the sea and his service, the *Matthew Andrews* left her cargo on Corsica Shoal instead of unloading it at a Lake Erie port. The captain and crew, fortunately, were saved.

In the long tale of disaster there was only one proved collision. It occurred on Sunday when the *La Belle* and the *Harlow* met in the blizzard. The *Harlow* sank near Peche Island, at the point where the Detroit River meets Lake St. Clair. The ship had a big hole stove in her bottom and three feet of water over her deck.

At the opposite end of the Detroit River, the *Victory* went aground while attempting to swing from the Ballard Reef Channel into the Livingstone Channel. The wind, still sweeping over the lower river on Monday morning, caught the steamer and turned her. She took a sheer which placed her high on the east bank of the channel entrance and had to have her cargo lightered before she could be released.

On goes the unhappy roll-call of the damaged, the stranded and the broken. By the grace of God and a bit of good luck, the *Centurion* crossed Lake Huron in the very teeth of the gale, although she was severely smashed up by the seas and lost all her hatch covers. The *Pontiac*, bound from Lake Michigan to Marquette, light, struck the end of Simmon's Reef in the Straits of Mackinac. She was able to keep clear by using her pumps, but she arrived at De Tour on November 12 with several plates cracked and water leaking into her compartments. The *J. M. Jenks* was stranded at Midland Beach, Georgian Bay, her bottom punctured; the Canadian steamer *Leafield* was abandoned and broken up by the waves on Angus Island near Fort William, and the *A. E. Stewart* met the same fate on the beach at Whitefish Bay. Fortunately, none of these accidents and losses cost a single human life.

CHAPTER 8

Adrift

THE READER may have noticed by now that all the various aids to navigation safety of the time were just as vulnerable in the face of the Great Storm as were the ships themselves. When these devices were put out of commission, some vessels still managed to stagger through, but many were wrecked.

Take that ancient emblem of hope for the mariner—the anchor. When a ship is being driven ashore, her very life may depend upon it. But at least a score of the vessels that survived lost their anchors, and many others were wrecked when their hooks could not withstand the force of the wind and sea.

Among those who survived the loss of their anchors, the steamer *George G. Crawford* had one of the narrowest escapes. She lost both her anchors but managed to reach the Soo after the Storm had loosened her rivets and opened her joints amidships. Her story, as told by Captain Iler, is well worth giving in full:

"I passed up by the Fort Gratiot Light on Sunday, November 9, at 3:15 A.M. At that time the wind was light west, weather cloudy. At 10:20 A.M. I passed Pointe Aux Barques. The wind then was northwest blowing hard. At 11:00 A.M., the wind was north and increasing in force. By 2:00 P.M., it was blowing great guns and still increasing. By 4:00, the sea was running so high and the wind so strong that we were making no headway at all. We were even having trouble keeping head to wind.

"At 4:30, it got to be too much. She blew around in the trough of the sea and I couldn't get her head to wind again. I therefore put her before the wind and checked to slow speed, but I had to keep ringing up half and full speed every few minutes to keep her out of the trough.

"The blizzard was taking our breath away with roaring gusts —deafening, blinding and driving. I got the impression that the ship could not live for another hour in such a raging sea. We couldn't see a thing.

"When we were running before the sea the waves were so large they would fill up the after part of the ship and go over the very top of the cabin, down through the skylight, which was smashed through, and into the engine room. The waves broke all the windows in the cabin and filled the dining room and kitchen with water. None of the men could stay in their rooms.

"During the worst of the storm our electric whistle gave out. The wires wore off in the cargo hold, where they go through the bulkhead. I couldn't use the hand lever either. I had to put the deck watch in the boiler house to blow the whistle. For fourteen hours straight I kept it blowing.

"It snowed for a solid twenty-six hours, the minutes marked by the crash of breaking waves. All this time we hadn't been able to see a thing, but were being guided entirely by the sounding machine. It gave us excellent service.

"I steered south by east for three hours, then south, using the sounding machine. I ran back fifty miles by log, then tried to turn around and get head to wind. But she wouldn't come any farther around than east by north one-half north, then she'd go back to east or west and roll.

"I used the chadburn to signal the engineer and I could tell the ship was laboring, for sometimes the wires would be so tight

I couldn't move the lever. I finally got her before the wind again at 1:00 on Monday morning. At that time we had soundings of ten fathoms and I realized with a bang that we must be below Sanilac in the pocket of Lake Huron and actually in serious danger. We either had to get turned around immediately and stop going south, or go ashore. I had the mate use the hand lead and I backed her full speed until the mate said her headway was stopped. Then I ordered him to drop anchor.

"The port anchor dropped first. We gave her the chain gradually to favor chain as much as possible. When she came around in the trough of the sea we gave her the other anchor and all the chain. Both hooks were then on the bottom. They were only there about five minutes before they let go. The port chain went first, about fifty feet from the anchor. Immediately afterward the starb'd chain parted sixty or seventy feet from the inboard end. We lost practically all of the starb'd chain.

"That happened at 1:10 Monday morning. Here we were in an awful deadly mess—both anchors gone, a blinding blizzard blowing seventy-five or eighty miles an hour from the north, and the ship getting into a pocket at the end of the lake where we were unable to turn around and head away from danger.

"We were in a God awful terrifying position. We had to fight it out. I decided I would keep trying to turn around until she went on the beach. Then I could feel as if I had done all any man could have done to save his ship.

"Our every nerve was on the alert watching for a clearing-up of the blizzard. Luck was with us. At 2:00 A.M., the wind shifted from north to northwest and a lull came with it. I got her head to wind immediately and headed north. We started back up the lake, and at noon on Monday it had stopped snowing and I was back up abreast of Pointe Aux Barques, which we had last seen twenty-six hours before.

"I tried to make an examination of the *Crawford's* top, sides and deck. But she was covered with so much ice and snow I couldn't really tell anything. The next morning, going up the Soo river I had the hot water hose put on and cleaned off the ice. Then we could see plenty of loose rivets and open joints amidships, results of the terrific strain that had been twisting her hull as we had attempted to turn her into the wind.

"I never would have believed that any storm could sieze a ship like the *Crawford* and hurl her about into the trough of the sea. Yet that is exactly what happened most of the time. It was the wind from the north that did all the dirty business. I never saw a gale on the Lakes to equal it, and others with whom I've talked since say they can't recall ever hearing of such a storm in the past. I was in the storm of 1905, but that was a summer zephyr compared with the one that raged over Lake Huron that Sunday. No person on shore could have begun to realize the violence of the gale. It's a miracle that we got through, but we did, and without the loss of a man."

Among at least a dozen other ships that turned up in the *Crawford's* condition were the steamers *George L. Craig* and *Farrell*. The *Farrell* had tried to anchor off Gros Cap Point but was forced to return to the Soo when both anchor chains parted.

When the steamer *Berry* turned up at the same place with the same story, Captain Balfour was shaking his head ruefully. "This is the first time I ever lost an anchor by letting it go," he said. "Crickey! That wind was something awful. We were lying under Whitefish Point when it whipped around to the northeast and north so quickly that before we could meet it our anchor chains snapped and we had to turn around."

Some of the ships that weathered the Storm could not have done so if they had lost their anchors. At least one ship was anchored only a few hundred yards from destruction. Most of them eased the strain by using their engines, but there is at least one case on record where the anchors were the sole guard against stranding.

The 319-ton schooner *G. J. Boyce,* bound from Westerville, Canada, to Chicago with a load of lumber and a crew of seven, had not motor power enough to be of any real assistance. When she tried to take refuge in Chicago harbor shortly after noon Sunday, she was unable to make it because of the wind and sea. Her call for help brought the tug *Kenosha.* The tug gave her a line, but unfortunately it parted, leaving her at the mercy of the wind on a lee shore. She dropped her anchors to keep from going ashore, and the *Kenosha* ran back into the harbor for a new towline.

In preparation for the renewed attempt, four members of the Old Chicago lifesaving crew went aboard the schooner to assist her crew at the anchors and to help get on board any lines passed from the tug.

The lifesavers' second attempt to secure a line to the *Boyce* was never completed. The wind and sea had increased so much that the tug was forced to run for shelter. The lifeboat also returned ashore, leaving behind the four surfmen to help run the schooner into harbor in case her anchors failed to hold—a questionable help indeed. The *Boyce*'s sole hope of riding out the rising gale was now in her anchors.

By next morning the gale was roaring its hardest and still the *Boyce* rode it out. Southern Lake Michigan was not the center of the storm, but the accounts of damage done in this area indicate that it wasn't a cozy anchorage, either. How the *Boyce* stayed afloat is a miracle, but she was still there on Wednesday, the twelfth, when the weather abated sufficiently for a tug to come out and take her into port.

The steamer *Cornell* survived also by the grace of God and her anchors, but she contributed one of the most hair-raising episodes of the Storm. Years after, her first mate said that "to narrate the details of the fight for life would only bring back the fear of death that possessed every member of the crew during the awful encounter. Recalling the terrible roar of the breakers would be enough to drive a man mad."

"The *Cornell* passed the Soo without cargo at 2:30 P.M. Friday, November 7," says Captain Noble. "We were bound from Conneaut to Two Harbors, Minnesota. Storm warnings were for southwest winds, but when we rounded Whitefish at 6:30 P.M., the wind was light southeast and the sky overcast. About midnight we encountered a heavy northwest sea with a light wind from the southeast. Until about 2:00 A.M., we continued to head into it, the sea running so high that the propeller wheel was frequently out of water.

"Then the wind suddenly shifted to the north, blowing a gale accompanied by blinding snow. The log showed that we were about ninety miles above Whitefish on the Manitou course. At this time the mate, who was in charge, was suddenly taken ill. I was in the pilot house, so I turned the ship before the wind while the mate was taken down to his room. The boat was completely covered with a thick coating of ice.

"After getting the mate to his room, we tried to bring the ship head up to the wind. The farthest she would go was east one-half north, which left her in the trough of the sea. She stayed in the trough until 3:30 Saturday afternoon. We worked our engines wide open but couldn't get her out. She wasn't taking a great deal of water on deck but she was rolling so heavily and moving broadside so fast that it would have been impossible to take any soundings with the machine even if it hadn't been frozen up solid.

"Sometime during the forenoon I realized that she was rapidly approaching the beach. I got the anchor out with fifty fathoms of chain. At 3:30 in the afternoon, we saw a tree on shore. Then we got out the other anchor with ninety fathoms of chain. We were able, by working our engines full speed, to get her head to wind, but not until she had blown far enough ashore for soundings with the hand lead to show only eight fathoms.

"This was at 4:00 P.M. Before coming to anchor, we made several attempts to get her headed into the wind by smoothing the water. We threw oil over by the bucketful, and all the time she lay at anchor oil was run through the hawse pipe, but neither method had much effect on the sea.

"She hung on there for eleven solid hours, during which her engines never once stopped working at full speed. I estimate we were about a mile or a mile and a half off the beach and probably five miles from the Deer River Lifesaving Station.

"She pounded very hard at times. She was drawing about seven feet forward and fifteen feet aft. We had eight or ten feet of water in the forepeak, tanks all full, and water in the cargo hold from number four hatch aft. Fortunately, during this period it was possible to get men aft to fetch a supply of cold food for those who were forward, although the catspaw and the chock on the port side were carried away, and the chain was held with the compressor.

"At 2:20 Sunday afternoon, the wind moderated a little. We hove up both anchors and left the beach steering north by east. While heaving the anchor, the wildcat was broken.

"At 10:00 P.M. Sunday, we encountered another raging gale. The wind at that time was blowing north by east, and we were east and somewhat south of Caribou Island. By 10:30, the wind had blown us off into the trough again. We let go an anchor with eighty fathoms of chain and, checking her to slow speed, headed her before the wind. I let her go before it, working her wheel just enough to keep her from going into the trough. We kept this up until 5:00 A.M. Monday, when a tremendous sea came over her aft. All the overhang of her after cabin was broken off, all the doors and windows smashed, and both dining rooms, the galley, and all the rooms aft except that occupied by the chief engineer, were flooded. The dining room furniture was smashed to kindling wood."

The vessel being light, it is safe to assume that her fantail was more than thirty feet above the water. For a wave to have done so much damage, it must have been at least forty feet high. If you've ever been tumbled over in surf by a six-foot comber, you remember the weight and rush of the sea. You might indulge in a little mental arithmetic; and if you get farther then figuring mass, consider the speed of a wave before a seventy-five-mile gale.

Captain Noble was at the moment too busy to play with figures. "We gave her more speed ahead, trying to bring her into the wind, but we couldn't get her any farther around than east one-half north—practically in the trough of the sea. Oil was run through the scuppers and hawse pipes, and thrown over in pails. The sea was running even higher than it had Saturday night, although at no time did the ship take much solid water. A heavy snow was still falling.

"At 3:00 P.M. Monday we caught a glimpse of the beach to the south. In desperation we gave her a full ninety fathoms with one anchor, but still couldn't bring her head to. The other anchor was then put out with a full length of chain. It held long enough to get head to, then the wildcat let go. We lost the anchor and all the chain with it. We had previously unshackled both chains for fear we wouldn't be able to get the port anchor up because of the condition of the windlass. With the chain unshackled we could at least let the port anchor go quickly in case we started for the beach.

"Luckily we were able to head her with only one anchor by working our engine full speed ahead, though it was a close call —so close that the sounding with the hand lead showed only eight fathoms of water. That put us about two miles off the beach between Two Hearted River and Crisp Point. The ship pounded hard at times and it was only by turning the wheel from hard over to hard over that it was possible to keep her from going into the trough.

"Between 5:00 and 6:00 Monday afternoon, the wind having moderated, we hove up our only anchor. We were too optimistic, for she immediately went off into the trough of the sea and started for the beach. It was an unpleasant situation. Once more we scurried to get that life-saving anchor over with full chain. We brought her head to again and were able to keep her lying there with our engine working full speed ahead until 10:30 that night.

"Then we hove up again and at last succeeded in drawing away from the beach. After going for about fifteen miles into the lake, we turned for Whitefish and passed there at 1:20 A.M. Tuesday. The wind was blowing from the northwest, strong with snow squalls. We arrived at the Soo at seven that morning."

Charles Lawrence, chief engineer of the *Cornell*, had his crew on duty seventy-eight hours straight during the storm. "On Sunday night," Lawrence says, "it was so cold in the engine room that the men wore reefers and mittens.

"At 1:20 A.M. Saturday, the storm really began for us, and from then until Tuesday it was a battle for our very lives. We couldn't head into the wind. Even though the engines were running full speed, we were gradually forced back to the south shore and blown eighty-nine miles.

"In some miraculous manner we escaped being driven ashore twice, got into the clear and started to run away from breakers that were rolling sixty feet high. One of these had swept down on the after cabin, carrying part of it away. The second engineer, who was in his cabin at the time, narrowly escaped death.

"It was a terrible experience for all of us. Coming down through Lake Huron later we saw the shores dotted with big steamers that had gone on the beach."

With such devastating fury to face, it's a wonder more masters didn't follow the example of Captain John Stufflebeam, who brought the steamer *Illinois* into Chicago, three days overdue, after a seventy-two hour battle with the Storm on Lake Michigan. Stufflebeam put not his faith in anchors nor yet in other works of man, but trusted his life and that of his vessel to a nobler creation.

"We had been up to Mackinac Island, stopping at all points

along Lake Michigan," story-telling Stufflebeam says. "It was only a freight trip and the boat was carrying no passengers. We had rounded the head of the lake and were ready for our return trip to Chicago. We left Northport at 3:00 A.M. Saturday. The lake was rough, but things didn't begin to look serious until a couple of hours later.

"We stood the rising gale and sea quite well for an hour. Then it began to snow and the storm broke all about us. We headed for the beach of South Manitou Island, but when we reached there found to our consternation that there were no docks, and it was impossible to anchor safely.

"I saw only one safe solution. We drove right into the land and forced the nose of the vessel up the beach. I kept the engines going slowly for fifty hours in this position. Their action helped us ride the seas continually smashing against us.

"At the end of fifty hours we were at last able to improve our situation. We succeeded after several attempts in throwing a line ashore, which we fastened to a large old tree. Then I could stop the engines and we remained securely fastened to that life-saving tree for the next twenty-four hours. Later we backed off and went on our way."

This is an astonishing marine story, and as far as we know, it's unmatched in the history of steam navigation on the Lakes.

CHAPTER 9

Battles for Safety

IN SPITE OF any laughter which might be occasioned by Captain Stufflebeam's choice of hitching-post, as it were, many a skipper would have been grateful for a tree—or anything solid—to tie to. Some crews were fortunate enough to reach safe havens, but only after taking a terrific battering from the seas. The crew of the steamer *H. W. Smith,* for instance, had a rough enough time of it so they were devoutly thankful to reach Port Huron safely.

The *Smith* had passed that port at 1:00 A.M. Sunday, and after proceeding a hundred miles up the lake was forced to turn back.

In making the turn the crew lost control of the vessel. She was helpless in the trough of the sea, tossed about for hours. Her survival was little short of miraculous, and had she attempted the turn a few hours later, not even a miracle could have saved her. As it was, she was continually pounded by the seas—great waves that smothered her in foam. They shattered every window in the pilot house, smashed in the doors of the after cabin and wrecked the deck house. The captain's and the crew's quarters were fully flooded and not a dry spot could be found on the boat.

It is hard to understand how this vessel, and many others that survived, could stand up under such a battering. It is equally hard to understand how the men who went through the ordeal stayed in condition to act quickly and skillfully when a chance came. A tiny lull, the slightest easing off of the storm, sent them jumping to their posts to snatch back control of their vessel from the wind and waves.

"But for the full speed of the engines and the turn of the wheel just at the right moment, there would have been another missing ship," says Captain Carney of the *Smith*. In just a few anxious moments, the fate of the *Smith* was decided and Captain Carney brought a living ship back to the safety of Port Huron. All that comes down to us of that epic struggle is Captain Carney's cautious statement to friends that "this storm was the worst in the history of navigation on the Great Lakes."

When the steamer *Susquehanna* came into port at Detroit on Tuesday, her crew reported an experience very nearly as frightening as the ordeal of the *H. W. Smith*. The steamer was fifty hours in making the short trip across Lake Erie.

"It was the worst storm I've ever encountered," said Captain Frank Bloom. "We left Erie Sunday noon and had been out but a few hours when the gale hit us—the same storm that swept Cleveland with such devastating force. It wasn't long before our rudder chains stretched so much under the strain that the gear was almost useless.

"Temporary repairs were made to the chain but then the rudder got out of alignment and renewed our steering difficulties. In this condition the boat was battered all over the lake and for several hours we had no idea where we were.

"The waves were so high that my stateroom up under the bridge was flooded and my trunk was dumped upside down by the wild pitching. When I did have a chance to snatch an hour's sleep I had to wrap up in my fur coat to keep dry.

"The vessel groaned and strained under the lashing of the waves and was on beam ends many times. This caused the cargo in the hold to loosen and it banged around inside the steel hull until every case broke open. Thousands of bottles of whiskey, coal tar, medicine, syrup and molasses formed a huge pool mixed with clothing, shoes and dry goods.

"I managed to get the vessel to Detroit by using extreme care. With the rudder disabled I was forced to check to low speed, and if the upper pins of the rudder hadn't held it intact, we would have fetched up on a beach somewhere. I hope I never go through an experience like that again."

Many ships and smaller vessels rode in what were considered safe harbors throughout the Storm, but found the wind and sea no less dangerous in their supposed security. The Pittsburgh Steamship Company had a number of barges moored in the east basin within the breakwater at Cleveland. The barges were anchored and tied bow to stern in broadside fashion with cables running diagonally from barge to barge. Cables that would have been secure under ordinary conditions were loosened by the wind so that the barges came together broadside with terrific force. In some cases, the bitts, strong timber frames to which the cables are fastened, were pulled right out of the barges by the wind. It takes a tremendous force to accomplish this trick. Because of this playful damage, three of the barges were blown up on the beach, and ten others suffered damages to the tune of $100,000.

The passenger steamer *State of Ohio,* which was moored at the East Ninth Street pier at Cleveland, parted her lines and immediately rode diagonally across the slip, carrying a fleet of anchored motor boats with her and smashing every one of them to pieces on the opposite side of the pier.

The steamer *Richard Trimble* was in the east breakwater at Cleveland. She had both anchors out, well bridled with forty-five fathoms of chain to each anchor—sixteen tons of tackle—and she was in good drifting ground; yet when she started to drift she kept right on going as if there were nothing to hold her back.

She had to keep her engines working full speed ahead to ease the strain on the chains. Although she had 8000 tons of water inside her into the bargain, she drifted to within 300 feet of the dangerous beach.

The steamer *Manola,* after reaching shelter, found that she still had a twenty-four hour fight for survival on her hands. "We passed Port Huron at 7:00 A.M. Sunday, November 9," said Captain Light, "bound for Escanaba with a load of coal, and drawing about eighteen feet at both ends. Northwest storm warnings were up and the wind was blowing hard from the northwest at the time.

"I figured that if it got so bad we couldn't stay out in the storm, we could readily get into safe shelter at Sand Beach. After making good weather past Port Sanilac the wind died out for about five minutes and then came this enemy without mercy. With no warning, the gale raged from the north-northeast, making a terrifying sea. At the same time it began to rain and sleet. I figured that as long as northwest storm warnings were up through the courtesy of the Weather Bureau, the wind would naturally go around to that direction again, making it easy to get into Sand Beach.

"The wind, however, held from the north-northeast and the rain continued; so it became a question of whether we could actually reach Sand Beach. We were extremely lucky to pick up the light about noon. By then we were really worried. In running under the breakwater, the *Manola* rolled so hard that both bilges touched, though fortunately not hard enough to start any leaks.

"When, after a great deal of difficulty, we finally made the breakwater, the government tug assisted us in tying up. We had three lines out forward on the starboard side, the best lines we had, a ten-inch line and a strong wire line abreast, and five good lines aft. We lay about five feet off the breakwater.

"After getting tied up we got to work getting the big anchor free and the tackle ready to drop it over. At about 3:00 P.M., while doing this, our aft lines parted with the noise of a naval battery. Shortly afterwards the breast lines let go, and then our timberhead forward alongside the windlass broke, making it necessary to let go of the mushroom anchor. We were then about fifty feet off the breakwater. We were still working to get our big anchor ready to drop, and it was finally ready when, lo and behold, the last line we had on the breakwater parted.

"We got the mushroom anchor into the water with all the chain we had. The ship drifted about 800 feet before the engineer got his engine turning over fast enough to hold her. Then we hove up both anchors and ran up close to the breakwater and dropped them again in a hurry.

"We succeeded in holding her by working our engine from half to full speed continually until Monday noon. Huge waves were coming over the breakwater. Although where we lay the sea was not so bad, there was a heavy current and a very high wind. Our windows and the skylight over the engine room were broken. While we were there, several sections of the breakwater were forced out of alignment and several other sections had the concrete tops taken off them by the force of the Storm.

"At 11:00 Monday night, I thought it safe to proceed, but in trying to raise our anchors we found that the two chains were wrapped around one anchor. It took until 2:00 the next afternoon to get them free."

Of those vessels which were on, or remained on, the Lakes, several were forced to ancient expedients to survive. In the misty past, when square sails and long oars pushed the prows of Viking ships far and wide across the seas, someone always had to stand in the bow of the vessel to watch by day and listen by night for reefs and other dangers. If, as many believe, some of those Viking ships were made of American lumber and launched on the Great Lakes, the waters must have remembered back across the centuries when they saw the second mate of the steamer *Alexander Mac-Dougall* huddled in the bow of his ship.

The *MacDougall* was on Lake Superior in the thick of it, taking the icy-green seas clear over her decks from stem to stern. They did great damage to the deck structures and made it impossible for a man to get anywhere on deck.

The *MacDougall* was a sturdy vessel, however, and doing all right, except for one thing. Captain Selee knew his approximate position, but was getting into waters where he would have to know his exact position if the vessel was to reach safety. And he couldn't see a thing in this raging blizzard. To see! To see! "God Almighty, I wish we could get sight of something."

He kept the mate busy on the end of the bridge working a deep sea lead, but that was hardly sufficient. The second mate and a wheelsman were sent to the forepeak to listen for the submarine bell at Whitefish. Amid the howl of the wind about the rigging and superstructure, the noises of the sea and the slap of the waves striking the hull, those two seamen huddled together and concentrated as they never had before on listening. They became all ears, for the very life of the ship depended on them.

They finally picked up the bell on Monday at 10:05 A.M., and had it abreast twenty minutes later. The vessel came into Whitefish on the submarine bell alone, for with all their prayers and wishes they could not see the port at all nor hear the note of its whistle in the mixed uproar of the gale.

There is an implement on board every ship that has played little part in shipwrecks since "cutting away the masts" went out of style and "manning the pumps" became the chief method of keeping a ship afloat. But during the Storm, many a Lakes freighter revived the use of this implement—the axe.

For two days and nights northbound on Lake Michigan the steamer *Saranac* plunged head on into the seventy-five-mile gale. The waves dashed over her bow and turned to solid ice, adding several tons to the weight forward. This burden, together with her already heavy load of freight, began to sink the nose of the *Saranac* into the combers, and she was in imminent danger of shipping a boatload of water. The sunken bow made her answer her wheel sluggishly and she constantly threatened to veer about into the trough.

At the head of a crew armed with axes, Captain Henry Durker led the way to the ice-encrusted bow. There they chopped away until exhausted. As fast as they cleared the mass more ice would form. With other members of the crew relieving them at intervals, the war against the ice continued until they reached Mackinac.

"The wind shrieked through the rigging of the *Saranac*," says Captain Durker. "There was a continuous roaring undertone of the seas and with every wave tons of water poured over her bows. Every window in the ship had to be braced with wedges to keep it from caving in. The steward had informed me there wasn't an unbroken dish on the boat. We had to eat our meals standing up from the time we left Chicago.

"Every time the vessel dove into a wave I expected the pilot house to be washed away. Had it been located forward, instead of amidship, it certainly would have been demolished. When we reached the Straits of Mackinac on Tuesday, the ice was fifteen inches thick on the vessel's upper works. The steam hose was brought into play dislodging most of it. When we were running into the gale, however, the steam couldn't be used."

Although she was one of the fastest freighters on the Lakes, the *Saranac* averaged but six miles an hour from Chicago to Detroit and for ten hours on Lake Michigan she averaged but three. She left Chicago for Buffalo Saturday night and arrived at Mackinac thirty hours overdue.

The steamer *Maricopa* arrived at the Soo with upper works and pilot house a solid mass of ice and snow. Although she had come through the worst of the Storm from Duluth with not a bit of her structures visible through the coating of ice, the crew had not been forced to form an axe brigade.

"I knew the storm signals were out," says Captain Story, "but I had no report from the weather station. I called the station by telephone and asked for a report, as I usually do, but the smart observer there replied that he was too busy to give it to me.

"The wind was howling when I left Duluth, but I thought I could run to the Soo and be that much ahead of the game. The weather was cold, bitter cold, and there was plenty of snow in the air, but we made good progress. However, the wind kept freshening and the seas grew higher and higher. At first they broke over our stern and then they began to wash on decks. The snow increased until I could see only a very few feet in front of me.

"When darkness came we found ourselves in the fiercest storm of our experience on the Lakes. The *Maricopa* was ploughing along in good shape, but the tension was awful. Nothing can touch the bitterness of that trip.

"The Storm came the hardest when we were about thirty miles off Otter Island, and we were forced to lay to near the Rock of Ages for several hours. Then I decided we could weather it through. We weighed an anchor, but I couldn't pick up the rock because of the blinding snow. The seas were terrible and I decided to use oil, which broke their force to some extent. Then we just came along to the Soo through the heavy weather."

Like Captain Story, Captain Hunt of the steamer *A. C. Dinckey* mentions the storm warnings. "We passed the Soo Friday, November 7, at 11:00 A.M. There were southwest storm warnings out when we went up and one of the linemen on the dock said they had been up for about half an hour. There were no storm warning notices in the canal offices.

"We went past Whitefish at about 2:30 P.M. and southwest storm warnings were flying there. We were on our course to Manitou and I had just taken a two-point bearing off of Stannard Rock when the wind suddenly started blowing a gale from the north. I pumped her full of water, putting about four feet in her cargo holds and fourteen in her peak.

"I ran for about twenty-three hours north by east, head to wind. It had been snowing heavily all this time—couldn't see a thing. Not knowing how far I had gotten, I turned around and ran back for three hours and then turned her head into it again, north by east. It took us about ten minutes to get her turned around. I went that way until about three in the morning, when the snow cleared up. I could see the Slate Islands and I should judge we were about twenty to twenty-five miles south of them. This was about 8:00 A.M. Sunday. The wind had moderated some, so I started again on way to Duluth.

"We had our whistle going continuously for twenty-five hours, but because of the roaring gale and blizzard I don't think I heard it once. She made good weather of it."

If Captain Hunt had left his point of departure a day later, he would have had a real battle on his hands, and his story, if available, would have been an entirely different one. In like manner, the steamer *Peter White* of the Cleveland-Cliffs Iron fleet, bound for Marquette, light, succeeded in making the lee of Grand Island before the north wind swung its double-edged sword over Lake Superior.

"We left Sault Ste. Marie November 7, at 5:00 P.M.," says Captain Kennedy of the *Peter White*. "At three the next morning, about two miles west of Point Au Sable, we encountered a heavy north wind and an hour later it started to snow.

"In the meantime the sea had become very high, so high that we had to haul the ship head to, steering due north. We kept headed north until 9:00 A.M. By this time the seas had become so big that the ship started to throw her propeller wheel out, losing her headway and going so slow that it was impossible to hold her head to. At times the seas would strike and throw her off five or six points. Then we would turn the wheel hard astarboard and let her go around in order to gain headway and bring her up head on again. By Jove, we had to turn about twelve different times.

"During this time, while heading into it, some of the seas struck the ship very hard, causing her to tremble and vibrate so much that she broke quite a number of her hatch sections, which dropped into the hold. The engineer stood by the engine, throttling it for twenty-four hours straight because of the way it raced when the propeller wheel was thrown out of the water. He had to use all the power possible, even taking the cuts off, to keep enough headway so we wouldn't go ashore.

"We continued in this manner, trying to hold her head to, until 5:30 Saturday evening, when the snow cleared up some and we saw the land about a mile and a half to the leeward. Then the wind lulled for a short time and we were able to make a little headway, gaining off shore at about a mile an hour. At about 10:00 that same evening, the storm seemed to die away, and we were able to get off about fifteen miles by 6:00 the next morning. Then it stopped snowing and we started for Grand Island Harbor, near Munising, where we arrived and let go anchor three hours later."

Captain Neil Campbell of the steamer *Sarnian*, which reached the Soo four days overdue, coated with thousands of tons of ice, said the Storm was the fiercest he had ever encountered in twenty-five years of sailing, even though his vessel was one of those that reached safety before the full fury fell on the Lakes.

"We left Port Arthur at midnight, Tuesday, November 4. My barometer was falling, but the wind had not sprung up yet. When I got around Thunder Bay Cape, it began to blow from the southwest. I saw my boat couldn't make it with the wind from that direction, so I went back behind the Cape. Five times I made an effort to get out. It wasn't until the next night that I got started. Thursday brought me as far as Jackfish, and I lay under the bluffs there until Friday night. I saw the lights of Mission Point Saturday night. I was forced to find an anchorage behind Michipicoten Island and didn't leave it till Monday, November 10.

"It was still blowing hard with snow from the northeast as I came down the lake. I could see two or three boats trying to make their way up, and a big fleet hugged the south shore of Whitefish Bay as I came by."

CHAPTER 10

No Time for Fear

CHIEF ENGINEER Edward Sampson of the steamer *J. F. Durston,* who played a vital role, along with Captain Watts, in bringing the ship safely home, has a few words to say about the Great Storm and the men who rode their way through it. Sampson was born in Quebec in 1881 of a family of engineers. His first trip on a Great Lakes vessel was as oiler on the steamer *Sultana* in 1902, a ship he helped to build while working as a machinist for the American Shipbuilding Company in Superior, Wisconsin. Six years later he became the ship's chief engineer.

"In getting back among the home folks at the end of a busy season," says Mr. Sampson, "we are always pestered with countless questions. The one most often brought up by the landlubber is, 'Don't you get afraid out on the Lakes so late in the fall?'

" 'Afraid of what?'

" 'Why, afraid of the storms, of sinking, of drowning.'

"The usual answer to that question is: 'A sailor that's any sailor at all feels far safer aboard his ship than anywhere else.'

"That question was asked me many many times during the winter of 1913–14, following the Great Storm. My stock answer didn't go over so good that year.

"There were many more questions asked this time: 'How did you do this?' 'How did you do that?' and 'What would you have done if this or that had happened?'

"In bad weather when the going is rough, the engine and boiler room crews are so busy keeping things going that they don't have much time to be afraid. They know all the things that mean disaster. They are constantly on the alert to prevent these things from happening and at the same time are thinking of ways to handle the situation if some of them do happen.

"After the ship is made seaworthy, the two most important things are the steering gear and propelling power. A failure of either usually means disaster. Our steering gear was under almost constant attention during the worst part of the Storm.

"The greatest danger and the one we feared most was broken wheel chains. The Storm put a far greater strain on the chains than any testing machine could have.

"When a ship is rolling and pitching during heavy weather, everything movable must be securely fastened, and watched constantly to see that nothing gets loose. Any heavy material or parts that do get loose can cause plenty of trouble, not only around the steering gear but in the engine and boiler rooms.

"Keeping the propelling power going presented many problems, all of which, fortunately, we were able to handle. It's hard to describe these things in any kind of order because often many of them needed attention at the same time. Keeping the machinery lubricated regularly no doubt helped a lot in keeping things going without any serious mechanical trouble. Hot bearings, burned jacking, clogged oil and cooler pipes were all closely guarded against. As it was impossible for the engineer to leave the throttle during the Storm, he had to depend on the oilers to report on the condition of the working parts of the machinery.

"The safety of the oiler was quite a worry to the engineer. A slight slip or misstep while going through the main engine on his duties—feeling cranks, main bearings, eccentrics, and cross-heads—would have been fatal. While this work is normally done once an hour to guard against overheating any of the working parts, during the Storm we checked all bearings two or three times an hour.

"For safety, with the captain's knowledge, we slowed our engine five or six revolutions, as the pitching of the ship and racing of the engine put a tremendous strain on the propeller and shafting.

"We had to throttle the engine during most of the forty-hour period. This means shutting off steam to the engine as the stern is raised out of the water by the heavy seas, and opening the throttle as the stern settles down into the water again. It's a matter of feel and knowledge and experience. The engineer has to be sensitive to every movement of the ship as she is tossed about from one wave to the next. Otherwise he cannot successfully throttle his engine. It's important that this be done carefully, as too much slowing down lessens the steerageway that must be maintained to prevent the ship from getting in the trough of the sea.

"A grave problem when a ship is rolling and pitching is keeping the bilges pumped out. During the most severe part of the Storm, we weren't able to put out ashes, which presented another problem. The sloshing of the water under the boilers and floor washed much of the ashes, along with coal, to the strainers of the bilge pump, clogging them up and allowing water to come up on crank pin connections of the main engine to the fire-hold floor. The water, ashes, and coal sloshing around their feet and legs made it difficult for the firemen to tend to their furnaces.

"Add to that all the noise of the wind through the rigging, the seas breaking against the front of the coal bunkers, the water pouring through the many small openings around doors and covers. All this made the firehold anything but a pleasant place to be in.

"Our greatest problem during the height of the Storm was in getting air for the furnaces. This is kind of hard to explain. The smokestack has an outer casing two or three feet wider than itself which is called the outer stack. This outer stack acts as a ventilator for the upper boiler room.

"The two regular ventilators which normally blow air to the firehold had been turned away from the wind early in the Storm and froze in that position. All the doors and openings to the boiler room were frozen, too. When the Storm was at its peak, the wind created such a suction on the two firehold ventilators that we in the engine room needed gas masks. The suction drew enough air out of the boiler room to cause a down draft between the outer and inner stacks, thus pulling down the smoke and gases from the top of the inner stack and making the boiler room and firehold unlivable.

"To overcome this we had to post a man at the fantail door to open it when decks were clear to let air into the engine and boiler rooms. He could feel and see the seas come aboard up forward, roll down the deck and strike the front of the boiler room. This was the warning to come inside and shut the door while the seas raced down both sides of the cabin, met head on on the fantail deck and ran out the scuppers. The door was opened again when the seas had subsided from the deck. We had to do this for nearly ten hours straight.

"Sleeping during the Storm was, of course, out of the question; sitting down to eat was also out. We were lucky the kitchen was on the after end of the ship. Those of the crew up forward had to tighten their belts for a long while.

"All the electrical and mechanical equipment functioned very well considering the disadvantages under which it was operating. A careful examination of all the machinery and equipment on our arrival in Milwaukee showed no signs of damage from the severe strain put on it.

"While all of us in the engine room realized that we were going through a terrible storm, we little thought of the deadliness of it till we arrived in Milwaukee. There we learned of the number of ships sunk or wrecked and the terrific number of sailors lost.

"Why we came through safely, while so many others were lost, is hard to answer. No one thing did it, but cooperation and attention to duty were probably important. A good boat, well loaded, a good captain who kept her in deep water out of the way of other boats, good assistant engineers and oilers who kept a faithful watch over the moving machinery—all these were important, too. Also indispensable were the sturdy firemen and coal passers down in the firehold. Under the most trying conditions and without fear or grumbling, they kept the steam up that was so vitally needed to keep the ship headed into the wind.

"Were these men afraid? Did they quit the ship on our arrival in Milwaukee?

"No, they did not. They stayed with the ship until late in December when she was laid up for the winter. And most of them came back again the next season."

CHAPTER 11

The Mystery Ship

EACH LIFE lost on the Lakes in the Storm of 1913 brought sorrow to someone. To those who mourned, it made no difference whether the seaman had been lost from the deck of a modern five-thousand-ton freighter or from an ancient wooden barge. To the world at large, however, realization of the extent and force of the Storm's fury and of the toll it had demanded in human life came only after many days had passed and boats not mentioned in dispatches began to loom among the missing.

The first report of an absolute loss was so unusual that it immediately focussed the attention of the nation. The entire marine world, even more than the man in the street, was astounded and shocked, for it was forced to believe what it had always thought impossible, that a modern steel freighter could be and had been capsized by the force of a freshwater gale.

Somehow—and to this day nobody can tell exactly how—a vessel had been overturned and, stranger still, had been left floating with only her keel exposed to the air.

The news was first reported by radio on Monday. A ship was floating upside down about eleven miles northeast of Fort Gratiot Light near Port Huron. There she remained, apparently transfixed, until she sank completely out of sight ten days later.

In that period she became the center of as wild and grisly a comedy of errors as the imagination can conceive. Because of her position, she could not be positively identified, and marine experts guessed every name missing from the shipping lists. Her size was guessed at by everyone competent or incompetent to do so, and the cause of her plight gave rise to some weird speculations.

While she held the front pages of the nation as "the mystery ship," she meant heartache and sorrow to hundreds of people. The lost ships were beginning to be counted; now a body washed ashore was identified; now a piece of wreckage told of a sinking. But many still hoped that some way, somehow, a life might have been spared from one of the lost vessels. The name of the "mystery ship" was not a sensational question to them. They wanted to learn her name so they would know if their loved ones had been lost aboard her.

For more than a week the ship lay in international waters between the United States and Canada. These waters are under the joint supervision of the federal authorities of both countries, yet no attempt was made by either to discover the ship's identity. Either could have taken on the work of investigating the wreck and determining the name of the ship. Such an investigation was especially urgent as the ship's position endangered navigation.

In spite of the many reasons for taking action, the Canadian government did nothing about the ship and the United States government did just enough to botch things up.

The U.S. revenue cutter *Morrill* was sent to the scene of the wreck and when she got there, was immediately ordered to return to Lake Erie. The reason given for this second order was that the *Morrill* was needed to assist the steamer *G. J. Grammer*, which was driven ashore one-half mile east of the harbor mouth at Lorain, Ohio. Actually the *Grammer* was resting easily on a sandy bottom, was in no danger herself, and menaced no one else; thus she seemed to be in little need of assistance.

To say that the transfer of the *Morrill* to Lake Erie shocked the marine world is putting it mildly. The cutter was desperately needed in Lake Huron. She was the only craft available for work at the scene of the wreckage. And there was much necessary work to be done—collision with sunken wrecks to be prevented, bodies to be recovered, possibly even lives to be saved.

When William Livingstone, President of the Lake Carriers' Association, learned of the government's action, he became a one-man storm in himself. He initiated furious efforts to uncover the cause of this action, and immediately dispatched the tug *Sarnia City* to the overturned hull. This was the first real attempt to learn the identity of the mystery ship.

When Captain Ely of the *Sarnia City* returned from his inspection, he said he had "found it impossible to make out the name of the boat because of the high seas and the fact that the vessel was lying keel upward." However, because he knew how anxiously the maritime world awaited any word at all, he started the great guessing game. "I think it's one of the big fellows," he said. "That's the way it looks to me. I think she was headed back toward the river [St. Clair] running for shelter, when she must have been caught in the trough of the sea and bowled over."

This was on Tuesday, November 11. That same day, ten frozen bodies were found strewn along the Canadian shore of Lake Huron, along with a lifeboat containing two more bodies. All of the bodies were wearing life-preservers. The lifeboat, and its oars, which were discovered farther along the shore, both bore the name of the steamer *Regina*. This was thought to solve the mystery of the overturned freighter.

Several other reasons seemed to establish the mystery ship as the *Regina*, one of the large freighters that disappeared with her entire crew. When the *Regina* had passed into Sunday's storm, Danny Lynn of the Lynn Marine Reporting Company remarked that "the deck the *Regina* was carrying looked dangerous. She appeared top heavy with a load of sewer and gas pipe which stuck way above the rail."

Although this conclusion was generally believed, some doubts were still expressed among the mariners. It was said that "the

Regina's bottom was painted green and the bottom of the overturned freighter was black."

Superintendent Dugan of the Merchant's Mutual Line Company, owners of the *Regina,* visited the wreck along with Captain
Thomas Reid of the Reid Wrecking Company and said that "the
mystery ship was not the *Regina.*" This further complicated the
mystery. Captain Reid stated that never before in his life had he
seen a ship upside down. "It's almighty hard to tell anything from
a boat's bottom," he said.

President Livingstone was in perhaps the best position to judge
the ship's identity. His tireless efforts to trace her identity were
continually bringing in reports and rumors for him to sift. From
his information he concluded that reports that the ship was a
"big fellow," a 500- to 600-footer, were probably exaggerated.

"I am informed by Captain Reid," said Livingstone, "that there
are eight plates around the vessel, not exceeding five feet each
in width, which would indicate the breadth of the ship to be
perhaps from forty to forty-three feet. The length of the plates
visible on the sides of the vessel might afford a basis for con-
cluding that the vessel's length does not exceed from 250 to 300
feet. Of course, I may be in error, but I feel almost certain the
vessel's length will be found not to exceed 300 feet." On Tuesday
night Livingstone said: "The fact that practically all boats of
the Lake Carriers' Association have been accounted for lends
strength to the belief that the vessel is Canadian."

The Canadian ownership postulate gained strength with another discovery made earlier Tuesday. Three bodies had come
ashore near St. Joseph on the Canadian shore of Lake Huron, all
wearing life-preservers with the name *Wexford.* The *Wexford*
was a Canadian ship, and since she was only 270 feet overall,
according to Livingstone's guess, she might well have been the
overturned ship.

At this time, three marine experts who were called for their
opinion stood firm in their belief that the mystery ship was the
Regina. They were Captain Carmine of the revenue cutter *Morrill,*
who had actually surveyed the wreck before being ordered away
by Washington, Captain Thompson of the tug *Sport,* and Captain
Plough of the Lakeview Lifesaving Station.

Said Captain Carmine, "I don't think there is much doubt that the steamer is the *Regina*." "It's the *Regina*," said Captain Thompson, "there is no doubt about it." Captain Plough based his convictions on his approximate measurements of the overturned hull. His measurement of the ship's beam was slightly over forty-two feet and the *Regina's* beam was actually forty-two feet, six inches. Little did he know that his estimate was over 30 percent wrong.

On Wednesday, eight more bodies were washed ashore in a lifeboat near Port Franks, Ontario; and it was announced that of the ten bodies found along the Canadian shore the day before, seven wore life-preservers with the name of the steamer *Charles S. Price* on them and three wore *Regina* preservers. But on Thursday an even grimmer harvest was reaped, and it was soon evident that the overturned vessel could be any one of many. Three bodies lashed to a life raft stamped with the name *John A. McGean* came ashore five miles south of Goderich, Ontario. This was the first report that this steamer was definitely lost.

That same day, twenty more from the same vessel washed ashore near the same spot, with wreckage from the most modern 550 foot steel freighter, *Carruthers*. More wreckage and bodies from the *Wexford* appeared at the same spot, followed by jetsam from the steamer *Argus*.

One can well imagine the eagerness with which Livingstone seized any chance to solve the mystery that troubled the marine world. What the governments of two countries would not do, private enterprise was prepared and anxious to undertake.

On Thursday a representative of the owners of the *Regina, James Carruthers,* and *Turret Chief*—all missing—informed Livingstone by long distance telephone from Sarnia that the little tug *Sport* and the services of a professional diver could be obtained on Friday morning.

"For God's sake, get them if you can," cried Livingstone. "If the weather is at all favorable, have the tug and diver go out and send the bill to me. You cannot be any more anxious than I to learn the identity of the vessel."

Sending down a diver to discover the name of the mystery ship was one of the hardest problems that confronted the marine men. For one thing, there was nothing that the tug could tie to on the overturned hull, and yet the boat from which the diver would be lowered would have to anchor alongside the wrecked boat. A heavy sea would make the whole attempt dangerous.

While the preparations for diving were being made, the rumor and theory factory was going full blast, producing some strange and wonderful material. One of the most astounding notions was brought forth by one Captain Wescott, who believed that the crew caught in the overturned ship might have lived for two or three days under the hull, as in a giant diving bell. Curiously enough, he had superficial backing for his theory in an actual case: the capsizing of the schooner *New Connecticut* on Lake Erie in the early 1860's. When wreckers arrived at the ship three days after the capsizing, she still lay on her side with her hatches under water. Yet within her there was still one person alive— a woman, wife of one of the crew—who was rescued and survived her terrible experience. The fact that she lived three days in the upturned hull was the talk of marine men up and down the Lakes for many years, much as the 1913 Storm is the topic today. It was considered one of the most remarkable incidents in the history of Great Lakes navigation.

Apart from such wild fancies, many technical marine experts were attempting to account for the condition of the vessel. While it is exceedingly rare for a freighter to turn turtle without being in a collision, there are many ways in which it might happen, according to shipbuilders. Earnest Ketchum, Secretary-Treasurer of the Detroit Shipbuilding Company, voiced the general technical opinion in a statement to the Detroit *News* that pictured quite dramatically the scene of the foundering:

"If the boat had been loaded," said Ketchum, "the upsetting would have been simple enough. She was not loaded, however, because if she had been, her forward end would not float at all. She would have gone down instantly and neither the spar forward nor anything else could have held her. Since she could not have been loaded, the only possible theory is that the high seas, which must have been running twenty or twenty-one feet, got under her and sent her over.

"Going out in a gale like that her master undoubtedly let water into her to be used as ballast. Rolling as she was in the trough of the heavy seas, the water ballast would rush from one side of the vessel to the other, and the more it rushed back and forth the farther over the vessel would list. With her rolling constantly increasing and gaining impetus each time she careened, a high wave getting under her would surely send her on over.

"Then the boilers would break away from their stands, smashing downward as she went over to rest on the inside of the deck. They would hold the after end of the vessel on the bottom, while the forward end which would have air in it would float and the force of gravity would drive the water toward the after end. This would leave the vessel in the same position as the mystery ship now in Lake Huron, stern down and bow out, with an even keel showing. The steel spar at the forward end would also keep the bow up and that combined with the air in the forward end will probably keep her there for some time."

Mr. Ketchum used the above observation to back his guess at the identity of the mystery ship. "It is hardly possible that it is the *Regina*, because she was loaded, and we all know from past wrecks and also as boat builders that no vessel will float with a cargo in her because any part of her is bound to be much heavier than the air that would be in her. A vessel navigating light, if she is water-tight, is like a corked bottle. So long as the hatches of the vessel hold, the boat will remain afloat; when they give way, the boat will go down.

"Many theories may be advanced for her sinking. She may have become top-heavy with ice, and turned over when an extra large sea got under her. In that event the ice would break away from her decks just as soon as she went over, and the air in the hull would keep the vessel afloat as she is now."

With all these theories given by so many experts in marine matters, anything sounded possible but probably none of the theories was right. Only one thing was definitely known: that a ship had turned turtle; that much was visible. How she came to turn will no doubt remain the great mystery of the Lakes.

Friday, the day set for divers to solve the mystery, brought more tension. Rough seas and added preparations delayed the attempt. More bodies were washed ashore near Point Clark lighthouse, twenty-five miles above Goderich, Ontario—eight men and a woman from the *James Carruthers*, one man from the *Argus*, and one unidentified—but no evidence was found leading to the discovery of the vessel's name.

At last, on Saturday, six days after the main bout, William

Baker, a professional diver from Detroit, was ready to go down beside the hulk and clear up the mystery.

"We lay near the wreck all night on the tug *Sport*," said Baker, "waiting for the dawn. We had everything arranged to make the descent at the earliest possible moment. I was ready at 5:30 and half an hour later I started down.

"As I went down I felt the ship's sides all the way for twenty feet. Then I lost contact but I kept on going down, expecting to run into the side again. When I discovered that I was too far down I started to come up and found the wreck once more.

"I ran into the pipe rail around the texas work and hung on there until I found out where I was. There was a round railing on the edge of the bulwarks. I went around this railing until I ran across the name. There I stopped and took my time.

"I read the name twice and then once more to be absolutely sure. The name was painted in black letters on white bulwarks— *Charles S. Price*."

History does not reveal how tasty the marine experts may have found their positive words once the true identity of the overturned vessel was learned. Not only were the men who had sworn she was the *Regina* sadly put out, but also all the boys who had flashed their superior mathematical abilities and expertness in measurement.

The American steamer *Charles S. Price* had an overall length of 524 feet, leaving President Livingstone 200 feet behind in his calculations; and he and Captain Plough, in judging her beam to be 42 feet, were cheating her of 12 feet of her rightful width. But worst of all was the waste of shipbuilder Ketchum's thrilling romance—the one which had the ship teetering from side to side like a drunkard, her belly full of water ballast sloshing about— for the *Price* had left Ashtabula on Saturday, November 8, with a full load of soft coal.

Once her identity was known, however, the *Price* posed an even greater question—one which has never been answered. She had left Ashtabula with a crew of twenty-eight men. She was last seen above water by Captain May of the steamer *H. A. Hawgood*, bucking the storm north of Sand Beach at noon Sunday "heading into it and making bad weather." From that time until she overturned near Port Huron on Monday, no man can tell what happened to her.

The first theory of her actual fate was accepted before her hull had been identified. It was brought about by the testimony of her only "survivor," former first engineer Milton Smith, at a Canadian inquest on some of the bodies washed ashore.

Smith claimed he had had a premonition of disaster when he left the ship at Cleveland on Saturday, the day before the storm. His shipmates had ridiculed him for leaving the ship with the end of the sailing season so near. Some laughed, some scoffed, and some made insulting remarks, but Smith had had visions of his wife pleading with him to leave, and of his family in Port Huron. Nothing could move him from his determination.

"My Gawd!" exclaimed Smith, "I might ha' been in her! I might ha' been in her! I was getting tired of sailing, anyway. I wanted to get away from it and I realized this was my best chance. I knew every boy on the *Price*. I am especially sorry for poor Arz McIntosh of St. Clair, our wheelsman. When Arz heard that I was coming back to Port Huron, he came up to me and said: 'Milt, is it true that you are going to leave the ship?' I told him that it was and he said 'Damit! I wish I was going with you.'

"I can see poor Arz now. The boy was having trouble with his eyes and wanted to come home to have them operated on. He had practically made up his mind to come along with me but said that he guessed he could stick it out for just one more trip. Poor fellow."

Smith went to Thedford, Ontario, immediately after the storm to help establish the identity of bodies in the morgue there. The first body he looked at was that of John Groundwater, chief engineer of the *Price*.

"That's him," said Smith to coroner Clarke. "That's big, good-natured John. How the boys all liked him."

"Are you sure that is him?" asked the coroner.

"As sure as I know my own name is Smith," he replied.

"Well, this man had one of the *Regina*'s life preservers wrapped about his body," said the coroner.

Smith was dumfounded. The mystery was more than he could fathom. Then the obvious answer dawned upon him—the *Regina* and the *Price* must have collided.

Groundwater's body was not the only one from the *Price* found with a *Regina* life preserver. Every additional body added its testimony to the belief that the two vessels had collided near Port Huron. Perhaps when the ships struck the seamen had grasped the first belts at hand, thrown to them when they landed in the water. One theory was that some of the *Price*'s crew had jumped to the deck of the *Regina* when the accident occurred. This theory was strengthened by the finding of two men, one from each ship, with their arms clasped about each other.

However, the testimony of the diver tended to refute this theory: "After making sure that the boat was the *Charles S. Price*," said Baker on his ascent, "I went farther forward to the stem to see if there were any damaged plates that would indicate a collision or any other damage to the boat. While going around I found two rows of deadlights forward on the starboard bow on which I was working.

"Then I started back aft. I pulled myself along on the rail all the time. I went to the after side of the forward house and found nothing there that showed any signs of a collision.

"By then the sea was coming up and began to toss me about. I had to give it up. I was under water an hour in all, and I investigated about forty-three feet of the starboard bow. I had no chance to go any farther on the wreck and didn't get inside her at all.

"The bow of the *Price* is being buoyed up by the air that was imprisoned in her when she went over. There are now two streams of bubbles coming out of the bow and there seems to be no doubt that the boat will continue to settle down as soon as all the air leaks out of her."

While the diver's story produced strong evidence against the collision theory, it could not be accepted as conclusive because of the limited area he had searched. Many marine experts still believe that the *Regina* will some day be found close to the vessel she struck, although Captain Thompson of the tug *Sport*, before going back to port with the diver, dragged his anchor around the wreck and met no obstacle. He told Livingstone that he "believed the washing away of the *Price*'s hatches and the storm-tossed shifting of the cargo combined to throw the vessel on her side, capsizing her without warning to the crew."

If collision is ruled out, what then? The two vessels, when last seen by Captain May of the *Hawgood,* were many miles apart, the *Price* just north of Sand Beach, the *Regina* fifteen miles south of the same spot. Captain Dan McKay of a D & C passenger steamer had also seen the *Price,* turning around into the trough of the seas about ten miles south of Harbor Beach and heading back for the St. Clair River. All this made for another confusing clue in the mystery of the *Regina* and the *Price*—they were sighted at about the same time going in opposite directions. How then were the *Regina*'s life-preservers on *Price* bodies, and what about that battered and frozen couple clasped together on the icy Canadian beach?

In discussing the wreck of the *Price* the day her name was learned, Captain Carmine of the *Morrill* said, "It is my opinion that the *Price*'s crew abandoned her at least thirty-five miles up the lake, or at a point opposite Harbor Beach. The finding of several of her crew near Port Franks would seem to refute entirely the theory of a collision between her and the *Regina*." The inference was that several of the crew might have been picked up by the *Regina* later on.

Against this theory of abandonment, however, was proof of how swiftly the *Price* had met her fate, as established by Milton Smith in his identification of the steward, Herbert Jones:

"There he was," said Smith, "lying there with his apron on just as he looked hundreds of times, when he was about to prepare a meal or just after he had prepared it. Evidently the poor fellow didn't even have time to look after his wife's welfare, which shows how quickly the boat must have gone down."

With no time allowed to "abandon" the *Price,* with no other vessel close enough to have collided with her, there seemed but one other possible answer to the riddle—that the *Regina* had seen the *Price* turn turtle, had run to her assistance, and had thrown over lifebelts and started to lower boats, when the sea finally overcame her in turn.

None of the bodies could give more than the mute evidence of a common death somewhere in the icy waste of black water. Their effects were only those things a man generally has about him at his work. The body of William McInnis, 20, wheelsman on the *Price,* carried a letter from his mother, a diary showing his daily expenses and a small parcel of money order receipts for the money he had sent his mother during the season—just what you might expect a decent fellow from a frugal Canadian farm family to keep about him. There were no hurried notes of terror, no fragments to tell of their last moments. They had been struck in the midst of life—it was mercifully quick.

CHAPTER 12

From Beyond

S O M B R E and silent, wreathed in mist and
shadowed by a leaden sky, a long procession of more than a
hundred vessels passed Detroit ten days after that fateful Sunday.
Ships of the Lakes fleet, freighters of all types, giant steel carriers
and little lumber steamers, slipped quietly down river, while from
the rigging of each hung, limp and damp, an American flag at
half-mast. It was a mute tribute to the victims of the Storm. No
planned demonstration could have equalled it. Multitudes on the
shore instinctively bared their heads as they passed, so impressive
was their mourning.

"It was the most remarkable sight I ever saw," said one spec-
tator.

The roll of lost ships was long—the eight ships lost in Lake
Huron, and the *Henry B. Smith*, which had disappeared into the
blizzard, and the *Leafield*, lost on Lake Superior, and the unhappy

barge *Plymouth,* abandoned in extremis in Green Bay and lost
forever. And waiting for the ghostly parade in Lake Erie to light
them safely to their last port, perhaps the *Lightship 82* swung
on phantom chains above the graves of Captain Williams and
his crew.

Of the twelve ships that disappeared only one had been
sighted as she took the final plunge, the *Argus.* From the barge
Plymouth and the *Lightship 82* brief dying messages came to
shore. There are no reports of the *Wexford* beyond "lost with all
hands." The same is true of the *Hydrus,* which sailed away from
Ashtabula on November 8.

The most modern of the lost ships, the *James Carruthers,* had
left the Soo downward bound through Lake Huron at approximately the same time as the *J. H. Sheadle,* yet the older vessel
survived and the newer one was never seen again.

The steamers *John A. McGean* and *Isaac M. Scott* were seen
some distance north of Tawas Point. The *McGean* was on the
direct De Tour course when last sighted. After that nobody
knows what happened, or when or where she foundered. The
Scott was just a few miles behind the *McGean.* She had sailed
from Cleveland on November 6 with a crew of twenty-eight, all
of whom disappeared with the ship. Captain May saw her with
seas breaking over her at about 3:30 P.M. Sunday, six miles north
of Port Huron.

With a lee shore, the *McGean* and the *Scott* were comparatively
secure from the northwest gale on this course, but what happened
when the wind shifted to northeast about an hour after they
were seen and both vessels headed into it is only guesswork.
Vessels taking a northeasterly course from the point where the
two must have turned might strike the six-fathom bank in the
middle of Lake Huron, according to Captain Hutchinson. If they
did, the tremendous seas would have broken them up before
the crew could abandon ship.

"We were to celebrate our wedding anniversary on December
16," said the widow of Captain Ney of the *McGean,* "and when
I asked my husband if he would be here that day he jested like
he always did about my 'solitary dinner,' for he never returned
before Christmas. 'Have a nice anniversary dinner and play I am
sitting opposite,' he said.

"Somehow Lakes captains' wives are brave. They're accustomed to storm stories, and, although the Sunday storm was terrible, I put away all thought of fear for my husband's safety. Whenever he was out in bad weather, he would telegraph me of having passed through safely.

"When Monday came, and no telegram with it, I wondered, but pacified myself by thinking that the Storm had been worse in Cleveland than up the Lakes. When I read the newspapers and still had no message, my heart failed me and I prayed for strength to bear my burden. I knew he had gone down."

The *Henry B. Smith* loaded ore at Marquette and headed out of the breakwater about 5:00 P.M. Sunday. Twenty minutes later people on shore saw her change her course to almost due north. A half hour later she appeared to be trying to turn around. She was rolling tremendously but got her head to it after a long fight. Immediately afterwards the blizzard shut her off from view, and she was never seen again. From the difficulty she was experiencing, we can assume she foundered fifteen or twenty miles off Marquette with her entire crew under Captain James Owen.

There is one brief report of the *Argus,* which sailed from Buffalo on November 7, with a crew of twenty-four. Captain Iler, fighting the *George G. Crawford* through the blizzard, saw her end. "I think it was the *Argus.* The storm got her around in the trough of the sea and she appeared to crumple like an eggshell and disappear."

Two days after the height of the Storm, the wreckage of *Lightship 82* floated into Buffalo Harbor and was picked up on the beach at the foot of Michigan Street. The flotsam consisted of a boat railing, two or three doors and several life preservers marked "United States L.S.82." A heartbreaking message, one of the only two ever to come from the Storm, was written on a door-panel in indelible pencil:

"Goodbye, Nellie, ship is breaking up fast. Williams." Captain Williams had written this for his wife. His body was found several days later. There had been a crew of six aboard with him. L. S. 82 had been a new steel boat, 150 feet in overall length with a 30-foot beam and had been moored by the government with four-ton mushroom anchors and with wrought iron mooring chain made under the most rigid specifications. Very long scope was given to the mooring chains and the strain was relieved by the proper use of the propelling machinery. She was stationed in Lake Erie off Point Abino, fifteen miles west of Buffalo.

But most tragic of all was the fate of the lumber barge *Plymouth,* and the seven men aboard her. The tug *Martin,* towing the *Plymouth,* cleared the Menominee Light Thursday afternoon, bound for Search Bay in Lake Huron. When they reached Lake Michigan they ran into the huge seas. The *Martin* and *Plymouth* anchored behind St. Martins Island until Saturday morning.

To save the barge from the rocks the tug towed it with its crew to Gull Island, where it was anchored. The *Martin* then apparently deserted the *Plymouth* and scampered for shelter to Summer Island passage, where it anchored. Abandoned and helpless in the raging gale, the *Plymouth* met her doom alone.

After the sea went down Tuesday, the tug returned to Gull Island, but could find no trace of the *Plymouth* or her men. Several days later wreckage consisting of hatch covers, cabin work and broken lifeboats from the *Plymouth* came ashore at Ludington, Michigan. Eleven days later a bottle with a dying message was found five miles from Pentwater, Michigan. The undated scrawl was written on the bill head of a Menominee firm and read as follows:

> Dear wife and Children. We were left up here in Lake Michigan by McKinnon, captain [of the] *James H. Martin,* tug, at anchor. He went away and never said goodbye or anything to us. Lost one man yesterday. We have been out in storm forty hours. Goodbye dear ones, I might see you in Heaven. Pray for me. [signed] Chris. K.
> P.S. I felt so bad I had another man write for me. Goodbye Forever.

The message was written for Chris Keenan, United States Marshal in custody of the barge. Keenan's body was found several days later on the shore near Manistee.

In all the long and tragic tale there was but one cheerful note and that was slightly mad. Abandoned by her crew after a terrible battering by the waves, the wooden steamer *Major* rode out the Storm without even a ship's cat aboard. The odds against her survival after being abandoned twenty miles west of Whitefish Point, already severely pounded, were apparently insuperable; yet a few days later she was still proudly afloat and was towed into the Soo by the steamer *Barnum*.

"It was only the careful battening down of her hatches which kept her afloat," said the chief engineer of the Mitchell fleet, of which she was a member. "About the only other thing that could have been done was to put in sealing wax."

But even this miraculous victory over the Storm had its sorry ending, for the tough old vessel had taken such a battering she had to be abandoned as a total loss.

Except for the *Charles S. Price,* not enough was ever found of the vessels that lost their fight to guess at the true tale of their last moments.

CHAPTER 13

Letters Home

I T I S C U R I O U S how most of us react instinctively with words to our experiences. Something happens
and instantly we talk about it or write letters to loved ones. Here
are three letters written by two seamen brothers, Earl and Gordon
Benford, to their mother, who must have suffered great anxiety
waiting to hear from sons sailing in separate ships through the
Great Storm. These letters are now in the Michigan Historical
Collection at the University of Michigan.

Toledo, Ohio
Nov. 18, 1913

My dear Mother
    Well it sure has been some time since Ive written you or
any one else for that matter. Personally I was so glad to be
alive that I didnt have any time for anything else. There
was sixteen ships and nearly 300 lives lost and the Carrell

rode the whole thing out and came to the ship yard under her own steam. She is greatly disfigured but still in the ring. They say that it was the worst storm that ever swept the lakes during the sailing season and I believe it I know several of the boys that went down and I tell you Ive got a kid brother with all kinds of brains as the Hydrus was lost with all hands. The Lord surely was good to us this time.

The Argus, Hydrus, Price, Regina, Cuthers were all lost with all hands and some others I forgot which ones and personally Im satisfied.

If I never git out in another like it Ive spent the last week trying to forgit it.

They say the Cort is here laying up but I hav'nt seen Cort yit as she is in the lagoon and were at the ship yard,

As ever. Earl

S. S. Carrell
Toledo, Ohio
c/o Toledo Ship Bldg. Co.

Lake Huron
Nov. 20, 1913

My Dear Mother:

Well you see I lied to you when I sent that card from Detroit going down saying we were going to Lake Erie to lay up. But I didnt do it intentionally I assure you. That was our orders. We started laying up Sunday morn. in Astabula but Monday p.m. about 3 oclock they came with a change of orders and we had to get ready and go to Lorain and load coal for Milwaukee then go to Chicago and lay up. If we get any kind of a dispatch at Milwaukee we oughto be started laying up again next Monday but cant say yet just when we will be throu. It will be early enough tho that is a cinch.

I got your letter and card at Detroit going down and the box of eats yeasterday coming up and believe me they do taste good. My oiler got up at 11.30 midnight and made a plate of french toast and a pitcher of cocoa and at 12.15 the Chief, Joe, Jock and yours truly had toast and jelly, cookies and jelly, cocoa and jelly, and jelly. Everybody enjoyed it. Oh yes we also invited one of the wheelsmen in to lunch. I guess that will hold me for a while as it wont be long now until I will be home where everything tastes good.

We got all that was coming to us last trip in the storm

altho we were in no danger at any time. We were having the time of our lives taking pictures. The only trouble was it wasnt half bad enough. The Pig sure was some iceberg tho when she reached Two Harbors, but a lively little ice berg believe me. One rail all washed over board, our hand and side lights were carried away and in fact everything that could get away went and it would have been as much as a mans life was worth to try to go across her decks but no body tried and she rode it out like a fish. I would just as soon start for the north pole in the Cort. She is a home but not a restaurant.

I suppose Allen is pretty tickeled to think he didnt stick to the Hydrus? Im inclosing a clipping from the Detroit Free Press with a picture of the Chief of the Hydrus. I guess they dont even know where she went down at least I have not seen a report of their having found any of the wreckage any place yet. I should think Earl would be ashamed to ride on a boat that would loose her nerve after she got clear up above the soo and turn around and go back to Lake Erie without a load. The Cort not only made her trip up but had unloaded a cargo of coal and loaded ore and was coming down again when boats got there which left Lake Erie five days ahead of us and now she is the last boat of the steel trust fleet to make a lake run. Some head liner this Henry Grunt boat.

I suppose Aunt Anna had a fit until she heard from Flop? Well Mother Dear I guess I will ring off for now. I will mail this at Milwaukee and we will only have a six hour run after that so no occasion to worry what ever. Love to all. Hopeing to be with you in the near future I am sincerely your loving son Gordon.

Toledo, Ohio
Nov. 24, 1913

My dear Mother
Your recd and sure was pleased to hear from you again. Id almost began to worry. I found out that Gordon wasnt here before I rec'd your letter but didnt know where he was. It was the Carey instead of Cort that came here.

I dont know wheather I can git a set of papers with accounts of the storm in or not but will try. You can certainly believe most anything you hear about the wrecked condition of the Carrell. We've got our smoke stack yet but thats about all that there was left on deck and there certainly was no boat any nearer gone then we are and came through. We're nearly broke in two. Anchors gone, windless a wreck. Houses stove in, furniture wrecked and just a cripple from stem to stern but were all here. We had our backs to the wall for seventy two hours and expected that about every hour would be the last but every man fought gamely and with one exception not a man showed the white feather and along toward the last we began to feel as though we wished she would go. Seventy two hours without sleep and practically without food and always under that awful strain. Sort of makes a man feel different about going. But we fought just as hard Monday as we did Sat. In fact harder Monday morning.

The house went in and Jack Kittell the first assistant said good bye kiddas. He has a boy 10 and a girl 6 and he was thinking of them. We all thought she was foundering. The Chief, the oiler and my self just looked at each other for about ten seconds then each of us went to our work again just as though nothing had happened and I know that they all of them felt just as I did about it. That it was the end.

As soon as things began to look as though we were going to git the water out of the eng. room again I went up and gathered up all the dry clothes I could find and brought them into the eng. room. Lawrence Kittell and my self picked out what we wanted and I distributed the remainder among the firemen and deck hands and we all prepared to make a hastey exit in case she shipped another. But we fought it out and at 1 a.m. Tuesday we dropped anchor in the Soo river and then locked down after breakfast and lay too at the government piers and took a 24 hour rest. The only anchor we had was a small one that she used to carry aft and we attached it to one of our deck cabels and used that. Both anchors and 180 fathoms of chain having been left up off Pt Crisp.

Allen sure was the lucky kid. Those poor fellows in the Hydrus never got one man ashore to tell the tale.

Your loving son

                                          Earl

CHAPTER 14

Aftermath

WHEN DARKNESS fell two nights after the hurricane and blizzard had ceased their destruction, the world believed it had heard the worst of the story. But when the news started coming into Port Huron and Cleveland the next day, the nation realized that the story had just begun. As the storm-blocked avenues of communication were reopened, the fragmentary information of the two previous days was succeeded by a veritable flood of tragic news. Each message added to the tale of wreck and death.

Ships not mentioned in dispatches before were now listed among the missing. Then, as days of quiet weather went by and several staunch modern ships did not reach port, it became certain that the Storm had taken a toll unlike anything ever experienced on the Great Lakes before.

Bodies and wreckage were being steadily washed ashore for

days. In some places the jetsam was piled five or six feet high
at distances of 1000 to 1500 feet above the normal shore line.
The largest concentration of the fragments was along the Canadian shore of Lake Huron from Goderich to Point Edward near
Sarnia.

With that morbid curiosity which is so common to mankind,
hundreds of farmers drove into the village of Port Franks for a
look at the bodies that had been washed ashore. Nor did they
return home empty-handed. Men living close to dangerous shores
have from time immemorial considered as their own the jetsam
of tragedy, and many of the curious quietly appropriated bales
of hay, canned goods, boxes of cigars, life-preservers, pieces of
cabin woodwork and the like, despite the warnings of Captain
Wiggins, a Canadian marine inspector. Yet none could possibly
have needed or used the water-soaked lifebelts or bits of wood
and metal which were carried away as grisly souvenirs.

These souvenir-hunters were to be condemned for more than
their greed. Their activities hampered the trained investigators
searching the same piles for the information awaited in hundreds
of homes and agencies. For a week the investigators kept up the
sombre search, hoping to piece together stories from the fragments of floating cargoes and pilot houses and from the frozen
bodies of the dead seamen.

Every effort was made by the Lake Carriers' Association to re-
cover the bodies of the seamen lost in the Storm. A complete land
and sea patrol of the shores of Lake Huron and Lake Superior
was organized with the help of revenue cutters. But President
Livingstone felt that his force was not entirely adequate. He
therefore wired the Michigan state game warden, William Oates,
for the aid of his department in the great search:

YOU ARE AWARE OF GREAT LOSS OF LIFE IN TERRI-
BLE STORM WHICH SWEPT THE GREAT LAKES LAST
WEEK STOP WE ARE HAVING CONSIDERABLE DIFFI-
CULTY IN RECOVERING BODIES OF SAILORS WHO WERE
LOST STOP

THIS BEING YOUR HUNTING SEASON WITH YOUR
GAME WARDENS PATROLLING THE FORESTS AND

SHORES TO SEE THAT GAME LAWS ARE OBSERVED BY
HUNTERS AS A MATTER OF PUBLIC INTEREST IN HU-
MANITY WILL YOU NOT KINDLY INSTRUCT THEM AND
ALSO HAVE THEM ASK HUNTERS TO CAREFULLY EX-
AMINE THE LAKE SHORE WHEN HUNTING IN THAT VI-
CINITY AND PROMPTLY REPORT THEIR FINDINGS STOP

IT WOULD RELIEVE MANY SORROWING HEARTS AND
WE WOULD APPRECIATE IT MORE THAN WORDS CAN
EXPRESS STOP

WILLIAM LIVINGSTONE

As soon as the newspapers announced the names of wrecked
steamers, men, women and children besieged the marine agencies
for details. The calls averaged more than a thousand a day.

"I appreciated the anxiety of those people who called up for
information about boats on which their relatives and friends
sailed," said J. Ward Wescott, manager of a marine reporting
agency. "I could almost see the expression of fear on each face
at the other end of the phone. 'Is papa safe?' was asked hundreds
of times Monday and Tuesday by childish voices."

All day long a steady stream of friends and relatives of lost
men came to Port Huron and Cleveland from outside points in
the hope of finding some inkling of their fate.

One aged man from Sombra, Ontario, his head crowned with
the silvery hair of threescore years, walked into a local newspaper
office and anxiously inquired for his son, one of the crew of
the freighter *Henry B. Smith*. "Don't you think there's even a
bare chance of my boy's being alive?" he asked, as tears came to
his eyes. "I just plain can't tell mother he's gone. It would kill
her."

Such pathetic scenes were re-enacted for many days. Dickson
Christy of Marine City, bent with age and supported by his son
Earl, came to beg information of the *Hydrus* on which his two
other boys had worked as firemen. Another pair of brothers,
Elmer and Walter Woodruff of Flint, were lost on different
vessels, Elmer on the *Argus* and Walter on the *Isaac M. Scott*.

Those whose hopes were rewarded were few and far between.
When the message was flashed that the *Hutchinson* was lost

with all hands, many hearts sank, only to rise again at the seemingly miraculous correction that the men were safe.

One father identified a body as that of his son, John Thompson, twenty-eight years old. His son was tattooed with the initials J.T. on his left arm and had a peculiar scar on his right shin. A body washed ashore at Kettle Point near Thedford bore the same marks and the features were identical with those of his son.

The remains were shipped to Hamilton, Ontario, and on an afternoon when the parlor was crowded with friends and relatives, the casket banked high with flowers, there came a vigorous knock at the front door, loud enough to wake the dead. The father answered it and, to the amazement of everyone, immediately fainted. There in the flesh stood his son. Immediately afterwards the mother fainted too, and remained in a condition of shock.

Everyone was outraged at the son's behavior. When asked why he hadn't written that he was safe, Thompson said he'd thought it would be a good joke to walk in and surprise the mourners. He had read of his "death" in Montreal; he was there at the time of the Storm instead of on board the steamer *Maple* as fireman.

To many whom the tragedy did not touch at all, the brief telegraphed messages, such as "CARRUTHERS IS LOST WITH ALL HANDS," were only part of the day's news, to be talked out in a day or two. To them such details paled before reports of the extraordinary fury of the Storm. One such report came from Port Huron.

In Port Huron there is a canal that opens into the lake toward the northeast. Normally it is thirty feet wide and eight to fifteen feet deep, with a swift current. The destructive power of the Storm had been so great that sea and wind lifted thousands of tons of sand clear over a large breakwater, filling the canal with sand for a distance of 1000 feet up its course.

People who read about the disaster from afar were perhaps the ones most impressed by the loss and damage statistics, figured to be more than 10 percent of the 880,000,000 valuation of the entire Great Lakes fleet. Of the total losses reported, about $3,000,000 in vessels and cargo were uninsured; so the net loss to the insurance companies was about $5,500,000. Of this amount, about $2,000,000 was on cargoes and $3,500,000 on hulls.

Of the total insurance, the Great Lakes Protective Association carried 25 percent; the remainder had been placed with American and British marine insurance companies.

Among the uninsured vessels were the *Matoa,* the *Argus,* the *Hydrus* and the *D. O. Mills.* Owners of these vessels, as well as the owners of several other large fleets, found it an economy to assume their own insurance risk, setting apart from earnings a sinking fund to cover the season's losses. Owners of small fleets are unable to take this risk, as the loss of one uninsured ship might mean ruin.

President Livingstone declared that the exact loss figure would never be known. "Personally, I know only of losses that have been reported, losses covered by insurance, and losses which fell upon the owners who carried no insurance. Besides these cases there are others which have never been reported, with which, of course, I could not be familiar. There were also a great many Canadian owned boats lost or badly damaged of which we have no record as to their value, their insurance, or their damage.

"Besides the boats that were lost entirely or were on the rocks so long they attracted public attention, there were hundreds of other boats damaged to a lesser degree. It doesn't take much to damage a boat so that $50,000 or $100,000 is needed to repair it. Many boats, when examined in dry dock, may have to be nearly rebuilt after such a storm. It takes months to ascertain just how much damage is done in cases of this sort."

Fortunately, the crippling blow which the shipping companies suffered physically was not so great as to put them out of business. The system that cushioned this financial setback is worth describing, for it is not generally known how the regular and seemingly unavoidable hazards and losses in the marine world are managed by front offices.

According to a marine insurance man who was quoted by the Detroit *News* shortly after the Storm, "When you read in the current reports of storms on the Lakes that such and such vessels have been wrecked and are a total loss, don't get the impression that the owners will suffer a material financial loss. As a matter of fact, it is quite generally considered that when a vessel is lost on the Lakes she is as good as sold—a freight steamer in particular, if she is ten years old or so. I'll explain why:

"All lake vessels are appraised at $42 a ton by Lloyd's of London. All vessels must be insured for the full value Lloyd's gives them, and, if a vessel is lost, the insurance collected amounts to Lloyd's valuation of the vessel. However, an owner is not required to carry insurance himself up to Lloyd's valuation. He may elect to take the risk of carrying insurance for say only 50 percent of the value. But when he does this, Lloyd's carries the other 50 percent.

"For instance, a vessel is valued on the $42 a ton basis at $200,000. The owner takes out only $100,000 insurance. The other $100,000 Lloyd's carries. If the vessel is lost, the owner gets $100,000 of the insurance and Lloyd's gets $100,000. If the loss is partial then the amount of insurance is prorated between the owner and Lloyd's. Of course, if the owner carries all the insurance and the vessel is lost the full amount of the insurance is paid to the owner."

CHAPTER 15

Accusations

BESIDES those directly interested in the fate of relatives and those to whom the whole sad affair was merely a seven-day wonder, a third group was profoundly affected by the Storm. This group consisted of those who knew the Lakes and the men and ships on them, whose lives were spent on or near the freshwater seas, and whose lot was cast with those who make their living from the Lakes. They mourned friends and consoled those about them who had suffered losses even closer. Of the three groups, the first was too stunned to act and the second was indifferent, leaving it to this third group to ask "why."

First the decks were cleared for action. Led by the Lake Carriers' Association, these people saw to it that all bodies recovered and identified were immediately shipped to claimants. They organized a disaster fund for the relief of the bereaved families which within a few days totaled $75,000 and finally over a quarter-million dollars.

Then they swung into battle with questions. Under the leadership of the Association and the survivors, they asked the question loudly: Why had modern shipping, modern navigation aids and modern safety laws been unable to cope with this giant god of gales? They set their faces forward to meet the next test the Lakes might put to them.

Probably the first outburst of indignation came with news of the removal of the revenue cutter *Morrill* from the scene of the *Charles S. Price* disaster. President Livingstone voiced the resentment of thousands, and voiced it all the more energetically and bitterly, no doubt, because of the strain he was under, working ceaselessly day and night, with inadequate help and facilities, to organize search and rescue work.

"God-a-mighty," said Livingstone at the time, "to call away the *Morrill* at a time like this is an unheard-of-stupidity. The *Grammer* [to whose assistance the *Morrill* had been ordered] is ashore but in no danger, while the derelict off Port Huron is a menace to navigation. With wrecks all over the Lakes every tug has been called away and it has been almost impossible to get a boat to go out to the wreck at night to warn other vessels away.

"Thousands of people are in suspense until the name of the vessel is learned. It may be the ship their kin are sailing on. Yet the government sends away the only means by which they can expect to learn the truth.

"Bodies of many sailors are drifting in the lake, but the government has removed the means of recovering them. Instead, the corpses will drift with the wind until thrown up on the beach, as a score already have been. They may lie on the sands in some deserted place and rot for all the aid the government gives."

With such a fiery pronouncement to quote from, the newspapers took up the hue and cry. The bizarre features of the story assured its being made known throughout the nation, and the manner in which the government acted was of course an outstanding feature of both news and editorial pages.

Really, the incident served a good purpose for the future of Lakes navigation, for it directed attention to the slipshod methods of the Treasury Department in such cases. And the newspaper publicity was effective in forcing the federal government not only to furnish aid to navigation in normal times but also to stand by with all its resources in times of emergency.

The keeper of Corsica Shoal Lightship felt directly the mass indignation at his criminal action. Although he had acted strictly in accordance with the procedure of his department, he was damned up and down the Lakes for years to come as a red-tape artist instead of a man.

But Uncle Sam did not escape with these two scars alone. The hottest fight was waged against the Weather Bureau and the heaviest cudgels taken up in its defense. Those who condemned it did so with vehemence, and those who defended it spoke out equally boldly in placing the blame on the masters of the vessels.

The fight broke out in Cleveland. During the excitement of the Storm, while the horrifying results were slowly being disclosed, popular opinion that the Weather Bureau "ought to have done something about it" grew with each succeeding report. Among those who knew the Lakes, the dominant criticism was that the Bureau did not clearly indicate the intensity of the storm and thus adequately warn the masters of Lakes vessels.

The Cleveland forecaster could not take all this criticism in silence. Stung especially by the blame attached to the Bureau for the loss of life, he gave out a statement to the effect that "daring and disregard of government signals are the main cause of disasters on the Lakes." The war was on.

"The statement given out by Mr. Alexander [the Cleveland weather forecaster] is foolish and untrue," said Captain Frank Pratt, of the steamer *James S. Dunham,* on Saturday, November 15. "The United States Weather Bureau itself is responsible for the great loss of life and property in this storm. The storm signals were not only inadequate but non-existent. No warning was given us along the Lakes and we didn't know there would be a storm.

"A week ago Friday night [November 7] I was with my ship in Duluth. My barometer was low and I called the Duluth Weather Station. I was informed there would be a high northwest wind and a heavy fall of snow. That's all. There was no

warning of a storm and the forecast given me was unreliable. The
wind switched after I had been out only a short time and came
in the opposite direction from that I had been told."

Captain Pratt's statement was a serious accusation. But frankly,
the weight of evidence is all on the side of the Weather Bureau.
To Captain Pratt's first charge, that the warnings were inadequate, was added the question of why the Weather Bureau did
not display hurricane signals. The answer is very simple indeed.
At no time had the Lakes region been threatened with a West
Indian hurricane. In sub-tropical waters, such as off Miami and
in the Gulf of Mexico, it is customary to display a special flag
to announce the expected approach of one of these storms, which
follow the coastline until they disappear in the Atlantic, seldom
even approaching the Lakes region. On the Great Lakes, any
wind with a velocity of more than sixty miles an hour was called
a hurricane. There was no special flag to raise or warning to issue
in anticipation of such a wind. In fact, there were only two warnings available: the small craft warning and the storm warning.
The former was defined as a warning of moderately strong winds
that would interfere with the safe operation of small craft such
as fishing, towing, and pleasure vessels, and usually denoted a
wind velocity just under thirty-three miles an hour. The latter
warned of winds "dangerous to navigation" within twenty-four
hours.

There is no doubt that the storm warnings were properly and
adequately displayed. Every vessel passing down into Lake
Huron from the Soo or up past Port Huron went right by them,
and every master should have planned his future movements on
them. In this respect Captain Pratt's statement is untrue—the
strongest possible warnings were placed for everybody to see.

As to the forecasts, they contained the warning "high west
to northwest winds." Every mariner knows, or should know, that
high winds—winds with velocities from thirty to thirty-nine miles
an hour—together with snow make a dangerous combination.
The vessel masters had the weather map before them and could
tell the nature of the storm and its direction.

Many mariners pointed out that this warning was inadequate
since similar warnings are given for every blow which passes

through the territory. They claim that extra precautions should have been taken to inform them of the coming gale.

The captains were much ahead of the times. Even now detailed accuracy in the prediction of winds is too much to expect, particularly in the tricky Lakes region. The Bureau could not have foreseen the unprecedented situation which developed on Lake Huron, usually a haven of refuge.

Rapid strides forward are being made in meteorology. Accurate methods of measuring wind, precipitation, and temperature are available, but the forecaster still has to take the responsibility for accurate prediction. In the Great Storm, it was impossible for the forecaster to be sure of anything more than that conditions for high winds from the indicated directions existed. It was impossible to state where and when the wind would rise from a velocity of forty to one of sixty miles per hour, or even that it would occur.

When the Storm sprang upon Lake Huron, it played the most terrible trick of all. Its change of direction, from northwest to northeast came so suddenly that the wind was blowing in one direction while the sea was running to an unrelated quarter. This change of direction, accompanied by the equally unforeseen rise in intensity, was not only beyond the powers of the forecasters to predict but was unprecedented in the recorded meteorological history of the region.

Captain C. W. Watson, of the steamer *George F. Brownell,* had something to say about this and defended the weather forecasters in this statement: "I think the Storm had been traveling along the regular storm track and after reaching the Great Lakes region was diverted from that track so suddenly that its deflection couldn't be noted until after the Storm was upon us. The high north-northeast winds were perhaps a sort of flare back of the high southwest winds of the day previous.

"My own forecast on November 7 was that the wind would shift from south to southwest, blowing hard from that quarter for perhaps twelve hours, then shift to northwest and blow itself out in from twenty-four to thirty-six hours, which is the usual course taken by such storms.

"There can be no question but that this was a freak storm

which defied even the fine equipment of the Weather Bureau. At 2:15 P.M., November 8, I received from the mail boat at Detroit a special northwest storm warning, and on passing Port Huron at 7:45 P.M., westerly signals were shown by both the American and Canadian weather stations.

"In view of this, I think criticism of the Weather Bureau is entirely unjustified. If old Mother Nature chooses to depart from the usual course without advance notice, the Bureau can hardly be held responsible."

Captain Watson's complete story of the weather at each point during the storm makes clear how impossible it would have been to forecast anything accurately in that meteorological confusion twice confounded.

"We left Buffalo with southwest storm signals up on November 7 at 4:08 P.M.," said Watson. "The barometer was low, wind south and fresh, with low heavy clouds. At 9:20 P.M. the wind was still south, fresh, and a moderate rain was falling. The next morning at 8:25 at Southeast Shoal, the wind was southwest, fresh with rain. The wind increased in velocity so that when we reached Bar Point at 11:40 A.M., it was about fifty miles an hour, nearly due southwest. The rain had stopped but the wind continued southwest and hard until about 4:00 P.M. when, as we entered the St. Clair River, it decreased in force.

"At Lake Huron Lightship, at 8:10 P.M., we found the wind west and fresh, the clouds very low, of whitish color and hard looking, and moving very rapidly from due west to east. At Harbor Beach at 12:40 A.M. Sunday, the wind was still west and fresh, with clouds coming from about west-northwest.

"At 2:30 A.M. the wind hauled north and increased very rapidly. At 6:00 A.M. it began to snow, continuing heavily until 9:30 A.M. At 9:06 A.M. through a rift in the snow we saw Thunder Bay Island, about three miles distant, and also a large ship headed south about three miles eastward, but we couldn't identify her.

"The seas increased very fast both in weight and velocity from 6:00 A.M. throughout the day. From Thunder Bay we held a compass course of north-northwest, passing Middle Island at 10:38 A.M. and Presque Isle at 12:35 P.M. As we were making pretty good headway and wanted to avoid pounding and racing, we worked at about our usual point, which gives a speed of twelve miles an hour in good weather, though this is well below the capacity of our engines.

"At 2:00 P.M. we were blown around into the trough of the sea, but with our large reserve of power we resumed our course in a few minutes, holding north-northwest until Spectacle Reef, a few miles east of the Straits of Mackinac, bore west about two miles distant. We hauled in for nearby Poe's Reef and had wind and sea on the starboard quarter until within about four miles of the reef, when we hauled west. From there to Poe's Reef we rolled nearly decks to.

"We had no snow from 9:30 A.M. until after passing Mackinac at 8:43 P.M., when snow flurries again started. In the interval the atmosphere had been perfectly clear. At 10:37 P.M. we passed White Shoal and saw Simmon's Reef gas buoy in the Straits. The snow then increased and at 12:30 A.M. we stopped and let go both anchors in ten fathoms.

"The snow continued throughout the night and up to 10:30 A.M., being so heavy at times the smoke stack could not be seen from the pilot house. At 11:00 A.M. we could see Lansing Shoal, about a half mile due west. The wind moderating, we hove up and followed the north shore to Manistique, and thence down the west shore. The wind went northwest about 6:00 P.M., November 10, and moderated to a gentle breeze by the next morning. The wind on Lake Huron from 9:30 A.M. to 7:00 P.M., November 9, varied from north by east to northeast by north, and at times from seventy to eighty miles an hour. The clouds traveled from north to south until about 4:30 P.M., when they came from the north-northwest.

"One effect of the high wind was that at times when a sea would strike the ship the spray would be blown as high as the headlight, which was seventy-five feet above the water. At other times, the velocity was such as to prevent the spray rising over four or five feet. The temperature fell rapidly to a low point and the ship iced up fast. The seas appeared to follow each other closely in series of three, which would strike with terrific force. I think few ships would have taken the punishment the *Brownell* got, in the trim she was in, and come through as she did, without injury."

Under such conditions it is hardly remarkable that the Weather Bureau could do no more than present the forecast it did at the

crucial moment. Captain Watson even expressed doubt that the
use of the radio, had it been available, to warn ships of the sudden change of wind direction on Lake Huron, would have been
of any value since those masters who, for reasons of their own,
were in the path of destruction could not have been warned in
time.

Why so many ships were in the danger area is a question which
is hard to answer. For one thing, the layman's contempt for the
Weather Bureau's ability extended to many masters. Having
heard what they considered false warnings so often, they neglected the truest one of all.

Many masters, too, trust far more than they should their ability
to make port or reach shelter when danger threatens. They alone
cannot take the entire blame for this, especially during the closing
days of navigation, with their schedules to be maintained and the
last few days' profit to be taken before the ship becomes a non-
earning storage responsibility for the winter.

On the whole, the Weather Bureau came out of the argument
better than its adversaries. While at the moment of receiving the
forecast there may have been no obvious presage of danger,
surely when it began to snow a look at the barometer must have
convinced every skipper on the Lakes that he was face to face
with a coming, if not an imminent, peril. Before the snow closed
in, each man knew at least approximately where he was. Did he
then lay his course for the nearest refuge or, as the Weather Bureau claimed, proceed on in the hope of weathering the storm?

Unfortunately, the political makeup of the Weather Bureau
prevented a real investigation which might have cleared the air.
Congressman Gordon of Cleveland telegraphed President Wood-
row Wilson requesting a Presidential investigation. According to
Gordon, the well-publicized inefficiency of the Weather Bureau
was not doing the marine world any good. "If all the charges
against the Bureau are true, it is a distinct menace instead of
a help to navigation," said Gordon. "I believe the situation demands a quick investigation."

The buck was passed to the head of the Weather Bureau, a
political appointee of the President, who turned in a beautiful
report exonerating himself and his department of any offense or
dereliction of duty. It was a case of an accused party reporting

favorably about himself. This was unfortunate, for the career workers of the Bureau would gladly have fought for their reputation. They can still point proudly to the fact that even their mariner adversaries admit the Bureau's day-in, day-out work keeps losses down by probably 75 percent.

No one person or thing should rightly bear the onus of this tragedy. Early winter is a dangerous time on the Lakes, and navigation never closes early enough to avoid its hazards completely. Closed within his comparatively narrow confines, the freshwater skipper can't "run before it" for days, as the saltwater master sometimes can. All too soon he must avoid an inhospitable and dangerous shore or attempt the dangerous narrow entrance of a harbor.

CHAPTER 16

Preparing for the Worst

ASIDE FROM its attempts to fix blame for the loss of life and property in the Great Storm, the marine world went into action in other spheres. Naval architects and builders, mariners, pilots and owners, all looked carefully into every phase of the Storm. Something had to be done to reduce the possibility of a recurrence of such tragic losses.

Captain James Watts of the *J. F. Durston* admitted that the Storm set him to thinking of possible improvements in the training of personnel and in various details of vessel construction.

"I did some thinking right after the Storm and I have done a whale of a lot since then. A storm like that would set anybody thinking, and I still shiver when I think what would have happened to us had anything gone wrong with the steering gear while plunging into the trough. Once there, I doubt if anything in the world short of a miracle could have kept us from going down."

Captain Watts, you will remember, had that very problem on his mind after forcing the *Durston* up the length of Lake Huron on Sunday. He has thought out a solution which, while it has not yet been adopted, is given here as a suggestion from a man who should know.

"I believe all engineers on Lakes freight steamers should be taught to steer. My reason for saying this is that during the storm it wasn't safe for a man on our ship to try to get from forward aft, and I imagine it was the same on every vessel on the Lakes.

"Probably not many captains have stopped to think how easy it would be for the steering gear to be put out of commission forward. If the cabin windows and doors are washed in, nothing is left to protect the quarter-inch shaft. If a couple of half-inch pipes are broken, the ship is at the mercy of the sea until you can get her under control with your steering gear aft. This is when the engineer would come in handy as a wheelsman. If one engineer, or better yet, two engineers on each boat were able to steer, a lot of trouble could be averted."

Watts also speculated on why so many ships were lost and the possible points of weakness of those ships.

"It's safe to say that every one of the lost boats got into the trough of the seas and was unable to get back before the wind or to head into it again. It would have taken but a few minutes for those waves to loosen the hatches and then 'good night.'

"I can't emphasize this point too strongly. I don't like to pass any remarks about the boats that were lost. But there is no doubt in my mind that any fully laden side-tank and water-bottom steamer that was caught in the trough of the sea for any length of time on Sunday night, turned turtle. I can't see how it could have been otherwise. The ship would start listing because the cargo shifted. The water bottom is nothing but a pocket of air; the ship begins to list, then the water bottom is bound to come on top."

But in spite of the disadvantages of water bottoms in storms, neither Captain Watts nor any other mariner would suggest doing away entirely with the double-bottom or ballast tanks. Their advantages as safety factors under all normal conditions completely outweigh this one disadvantage. In the shallow channels and treacherous waters of the Lakes, the extra bottom and the water-tight compartments are essential to eliminating losses from broken outer hulls.

"Many other lost vessels," Watts continues, "probably filled and sank when their hatches came loose. There is too much dependence put on the weight of the hatches, which is expected to hold them down on the coaming. Frequently they lift up from the coaming, anyway. And all cargo holds should have a vent to let air escape when a vessel is rolling."

More and more modern ship construction follows his advice. As a safety factor, hatch control is doubly important on the Lakes freighter, whose construction is determined by the heavy cargo demands made upon her. With the pilot house at the tip of the bow and the powerhouse at the very stern, her entire midships is one great hold for the quick handling of bulk cargoes. This hold is protected by from twelve to as many as forty hatches, compared to the ocean freighter's usual two. The unusual number of hatches makes it necessary to take great care in their construction so as to afford the greatest possible safety.

Hatches are, and always have been, the most vulnerable part of the vessel. The universal practice for years had been to close the hatchway openings in the weather decks with wooden covers, covered by tarpaulins. For many years no thought was given to improvements because hatches were easy to repair or renew, since wood could be obtained easily at any and every port. But during heavy weather tarpaulins were easily torn off, and many times the first smashing wave over the decks did the worst damage. It struck the side coamings, deflecting and forcing them upwards and the wooden covers just floated off overboard or fell into the hold. Subsequent waves completed the destruction.

Most of the freighters in 1913 were fitted with twelve-inch coamings and wooden hatch covers. For many years, these have been superseded by the sectional telescoping steel hatch cover, practically the standard for modern bulk freighters. Hatches of this type are opened and closed by steam winches with wire cables attached to the centerline sections. These sections, when closed, fit loosely and for watertightness must be covered by tarpaulins properly battened down, which act as a seal. In all attempts to improve on this type of hatch, the problem has been speed and ease of handling, proper stowage of covers and, if possible, the elimination of tarpaulins for watertightness.

The latest type of hatch cover on the Lakes freighters is a one-piece steel cover handled by a low overhead traveling bridge crane. This six and a half ton crane runs fore-and-aft the entire length of the deck on rails, one fitted to the deck on each side. The crane lifts the covers clear of the hatches and transfers them to stowage locations between hatches. Each cover can be removed or replaced in one minute with one man operating the crane and two men serving the hoisting hooks. This means that in a modern freighter with sixteen large hatch openings, all hatches can be opened or closed in thirty minutes with a minimum of light hand labor. There is also a substantial saving in operation, since no tarpaulins are needed. These covers have proved to be completely watertight.

But ship construction and the training of personnel were not to account for the greatest strides made towards safety for storm-tossed vessels. When the next great test came, an entirely new safety device faced the freshwater storm.

This new device came in as an older one went out. For years, lightships had been considered superior to lighthouses in many locations. They provided both light and sound signals; a vessel might steer directly for them in safety as long as collision was avoided; and they could be moved with changing conditions and shifting channels. However, as we have seen, if one was moved by the force of a storm it might become a menace instead of an aid. The government, for this reason and because of their expense, has eliminated all lightships from the Lakes.

To replace them, modern science and technics have given the Lakes masters a goal they can steer for in complete confidence, an immovable guide across waters shrouded in fog, clogged with snow, or hidden in the blackness of the night. The greatest safety factor on the Lakes today is the radio beacon, accurate to a compass degree in all weather and audible for the entire length of each course marked.

In 1921, the United States opened experiments near the harbor of New York City with three stations. They were the first successful stations in regular service. Four years later the first stations on the Great Lakes were established. Since 1921, the number of radio beacon stations all over the world has increased to more than 500, of which fifty-one serve the Great Lakes. Direction finders on commercial ships have increased from 291 in 1924 to more than 10,000 today. Since 1937, they have been installed on almost all Lakes freighters and are rapidly becoming standard equipment on even the smaller pleasure craft.

The development of this wonderful marine safety aid was not unattended by the traditional growing pains. As the beacons became more numerous, they could no longer use the same frequency without interfering with each other. When this condition became so bad that something had to be done about it, a thirty kilocycle band of frequencies was reserved for marine radio beacons exclusively. This band is within the limits of 285 and 315 kilocycles.

The band soon became inadequate, however, and in order to take care of the situation an elaborate system of timing was instituted. Since it was impossible to allocate a new band of frequencies, it was found necessary to operate three separate radio beacons on each available frequency, emitting signals each in sequence for one minute out of every three. This complicated timing system synchronized all the radio beacons in the United States.

This is not as convenient to the mariner as if all radio beacons operated without interruption, but it has made it possible to establish a larger number of beacons than would otherwise have been possible. Further expansion of the band now allocated is limited by the demands of other public services, such as commercial broadcasting, ship and air transport communication, military communication, and so forth. Receivers have kept pace with the development of the beam. Where early receivers had difficulty in separating two signals many kilocycles apart, modern ones have the most critical selectivity.

It is now possible to take great circle bearings from a radio beacon. A shielded, rotating loop, mounted above the pilot house, picks up the signal. When at right angles to the direction from which the signal comes, the signal is zero or nearly so. As the plane of the loop approaches the direction of the signal, volume increases to a maximum "on the beam." The motion of this loop is controlled from the pilot house by means of a hand wheel. On this wheel a pointer on a compass scale is calibrated to show the true direction at zero or minimum signal. The whole apparatus has to be carefully calibrated to compensate for the magnetic attraction of the steel hull, stacks and so forth, just as the ship's magnetic compass is corrected.

It is also possible by simple trigonometry to fix the vessel's position by use of the radio beacon. Snow or fog can dim the brightest light, but neither of these dangers can touch the radio beacon. With it the navigator can keep constant check on his position in the thickest blizzard.

"Things have improved for the crews during the past decade," says Captain Robert Edelman, "and for skippers also. The ships are now gyro-equipped and these gyros are a great deal more reliable than the old style magnetic compass. They are not affected by the ore deposits along Lake Superior. Most ships have ship-to-shore telephones. That's American efficiency. You can notify a dock just what minute you'll arrive and the dock gangs will be ready to start work the instant the ship is tied up.

"And another boon to the captain is the radio direction finder. With that he can take a cross bearing and know within a few inches the exact spot he occupies on a few thousand square miles of water. The radio direction finder has eliminated the necessity of trailing a log. Practically all Lakes boats have discontinued the use of a log."

It was fortunate that the radio beacon was in regular use on the Great Lakes by 1937. Not long after that it was called upon to face its first man-sized test, the storm of November 1940.

CHAPTER 17

Return Bout

SINCE THE Great Storm, there have been several gales on the Great Lakes, all striking during the closing days of navigation and all accompanied by shipwrecks, disappearances, strandings and loss of life; but it was not until November 12, 1940, that a storm occurred almost as violent as that of 1913.

Captain Harold B. McCool of the automobile carrier *Crescent City* has transcribed from her logbook the main details of his vessel's experience on Lake Superior and added comments of his own:

"The logbook of the *Crescent City* shows we left the Soo locks for Duluth Light at 11:25 A.M., November 10, with a northwest wind blowing at the time. There was a small craft storm signal up at the weather station, but as a rule we don't pay much attention to those signals.

"After passing Whitefish Point at 3:00 P.M., we made our course for Michipicoten Island because the weather report had forecast northeast winds. After passing Michipicoten at 9:00 P.M., we headed for Otter Island. Arriving there two hours later, we found that the wind had backed up to east-northeast and had increased to thirty-five miles an hour. With the wind from that direction we had to change our course and go right up the middle of the lake to Devil's Island.

"About 6:00 P.M. on November 11, I knew we were in for something. We were only fifteen miles east-northeast of Devil's Island when the wind flattened out and it stopped raining. After fifteen minutes of calm it started to blow great guns from the north. With the temperature and barometer dropping together, I knew the lull had been just the famous 'calm before the storm.'

"There had been a heavy sea from east-northeast following us all day, but the change of wind to north made a sea heading at us from that direction. We finally altered our course to head into it. Yet every now and then the old east-northeast sea would come and take charge of us from that quarter. When it did, we were in serious danger—the ship would nearly turn over.

"About 10:00 that same night, I had to turn and run before it. I had overrun my time and log for a course which brought me dangerously close to the shore, and it was snowing so thickly I couldn't have seen the smokestack if it had been the middle of the day.

"If we had been in danger before, it was mild compared to our peril when we turned and got into the trough of the seas. I never knew a ship could roll so far and not go over. In fact, I didn't believe it possible while it was actually happening. Each time she swung through that arc I was sure she'd just keep on going. We lost thirty-six automobiles from our weather deck load overboard, and counted ourselves mighty lucky not to lose the ship itself with every man on board.

"We got the full force of the storm about 11:00 P.M. The wind was blowing seventy-five miles an hour. The seas were regular tidal waves tumbling from the north, and it's a great wonder that any automobiles were still on deck when we arrived in Duluth.

"We had to turn again after we had run before it a short while. Remember, the lake is only twenty-five miles wide at that point, and we were considerably cramped for real maneuvering space.

"By 1:00 A.M. on the twelfth, it had let up snowing and the wind was backing to westward. That gave us a chance to haul up for Duluth. About 5:00 A.M., after the sea had been letting up for about an hour, we sighted Split Rock Light and after getting our bearings on it we knew just where we were. At 7:30 A.M., we were about eight miles off Two Harbors, twenty-five miles from Duluth. We arrived there three hours later, covered with ice."

Of the other survivors, the oil tankers *New Haven Socony* and *Crudoil* took the worst beatings. The *Socony* reached Chicago covered with ice and minus one lifeboat, one raft and the pilot house, her compass dead, navigation charts washed away and the radio on the blink. As Bos'n Frank Myers put it, she'd "been through hell and all over Lake Michigan besides." The *Crudoil* luckily made port at Sturgeon Bay, Wisconsin, in spite of disabled steering gear and six feet of water in her hold.

Many freighters were driven ashore or stranded and badly damaged. Among these was the Canadian pulpwood carrier *Novadoc,* which broke up completely when she was driven ashore near Pentwater, Michigan. In the battering, two of her crew of nineteen were lost before the survivors were taken off by the tug *Three Brothers.* The crew of the steel steamer *Sinaloa,* blown ashore and abandoned in the Big Bay de Noc, was most stirringly rescued. Fishermen from nearby Garden, Michigan, put out to the aid of the *Sinaloa* without waiting for the arrival of the Coast Guard. They had already removed twenty-two of the crew members when their boat capsized in the seething waters. The wet and freezing seamen saved themselves by grasping a line which had been rigged up from ship to shore, and pulling themselves hand over hand to safety. The Coast Guard then successfully completed the rescue of the crew.

Again, there were bodies washed ashore—sixteen of them— near Ludington and Pentwater, wearing lifebelts of the steamers *William B. Davock* and *Anna C. Minch.* The *Davock's* resting place is unknown, but the *Minch* sank only 400 feet off shore near Pentwater. The crews of both these vessels totaled fifty-seven. Together with the two lost from the *Novadoc* and eight from the tugs *Richard H.* and *Indian* of South Haven, Michigan, they account for the total storm loss of sixty-seven lives.

But the most important story of the 1940 storm is that, beyond the brief details given, there *is* no story. Given a gale almost as violent as that of 1913 and a greater number of ships to prey on, the god of gales could not amass the same total of victims.

The best stories are those that would have little interest for the reader—the stories of ships that safely made port "on the beam" in spite of the blizzard, of masters who knew exactly where they were and how to reach safety in spite of the smother, and of men who knew that they were securely linked with the land by an invisible line stronger than the thickest hawser or chain.

No one can say that there will never again be lives lost and vessels crushed. As long as men go down to the sea in ships there are dangers, no matter what aids science may bring. As long as the earth keeps rolling, the waters will periodically be stirred to wrath, and the men aboard ship will be subject to the fickle anger of the seas.

But as long as the human animal trusts his goods and his life to steel bottoms on the Great Lakes, it is extremely unlikely he will ever suffer what he did during those terrible November days of 1913. The ingenuity of the sailing man grows apace and his memory is long enough to recall what the Lakes have done and can do again if he neglects his skill and forgets his cunning.

1. Statistics on Vessels Totally Destroyed*

Vessel	Gross Tonnage	Length Over All	Beam	When Built	Value of Vessel	Vessel Insured For	Cargo	Cargo Insured For	Lives Lost	Location of Loss	Owner
Argus	4707	436'	50'	1903	$136,000		Coal	$15,000	24	Lake Huron	Interlake Steamship Co., Cleveland
Charles S. Price	6322	524'	54'	1910	340,000	$322,400	Coal	21,700	28	Lake Huron	Mahoning Steamship Co., M. A. Hanna & Co., Mgr., Cleveland
Halsted (barge)	496	191'	32'	1873	5,000					Green Bay, Lake Mich.	Soper Lumber Co., W. E. Holems & Co., Mgr., Chicago
H. B. Smith	6631	545'	55'	1906	350,000	338,200	Ore	38,000	23	Lake Superior	Acme Transit Co., Hawgood & Co., Mgr., Cleveland
Howard M. Hanna, Jr.	5905	500'	54'	1908	315,000	301,200	Coal	20,000		Pointe Aux Barques, Lake Huron	Hanna Transit Co., W. C. Richardson & Co., Mgr., Cleveland
Hydrus	4713	436'	50'	1903	136,000		Ore	28,000	24	Lake Huron	Interlake Steamship Co., Cleveland
Isaac M. Scott	6372	524'	54'	1909	340,000	325,000	Coal	20,000	28	Lake Huron	Virginia Steamship Co., M. A. Hanna & Co., Mgr., Cleveland
James Carruthers	7862	550'	58'	1913	410,000	400,900	Grain	350,000	24 †	Lake Huron	St. Lawrence & Chicago Steam Navigation Co., Ltd., Toronto
John A. McGean	5100	452'	52'	1908	240,000	227,700	Coal	17,900	23	Lake Huron	Pioneer Steamship Co., Hutchinson & Co., Mgr., Cleveland
L. C. Waldo	4466	472'	48'	1896	250,000	227,700	Ore	23,000		Manitou Island, Lake Superior	Roby Transp. Co., L. C. Waldo, Mgr., Detroit
Leafield	1453	269'	35.25'	1892	100,000	74,100	Steel Rails	70,000	18	Angus Island, Lake Superior	Algoma Central S. S. Line, Sault Ste. Marie, Ont.

1. Statistics on Vessels Totally Destroyed (Cont.)

Vessel	Gross Tonnage	Length Over All	Beam	When Built	Value of Vessel	Vessel Insured For	Cargo	Cargo Insured For	Lives Lost	Location of Loss	Owner
Lightship 82	180	105'	21'	1912	25,000				6	Point Abino, Lake Erie	Lighthouse Bureau, U.S. Government
Louisiana	1929	287'	39'	1887	20,000	15,000				Washington Island, Lake Michigan	Thompson Steamship Co., J. R. Davock, Mgr., Cleveland
Major	1864	303'	41'	1889	28,000	25,000	Coal	12,000		Whitefish Pt., Lake Superior	Cleveland Steamship Co, John Mitchell, Mgr.
Matoa	2311	310'	40'	1890	117,900		Coal	12,000		Pointe Aux Barques, Lake Huron	Pittsburgh Steamship Co, Cleveland
Plymouth (barge)	776	225'	35'	1854	5,000				7	Gull Island, Lake Michigan	McKinnon & Scott, Menominee, Michigan
Regina	1956	269'	42.5'	1907	125,000	99,800			25 †	Lake Huron	Merchants Mutual Line Co., Toronto
Turret Chief	1881	273'	44'	1896	100,000					Copper Harbor, Lake Superior	Canadian Lake & Ocean Navigation Co, Toronto
Wexford	2104	270'	40'	1883	125,000	107,300	Steel Rails		18 †	Lake Huron	Western Steamship Co, Ltd., Toronto

* Source: Lake Carriers' Association *Annual Report, 1913* (Cleveland, 1913).
† The figures on loss of life given by the Lake Carriers' Association were: *Carruthers*, 19; *Regina*, 15; and *Wexford*, 17. The correct figures, given in the table above, were obtained from the Canadian Department of Transport by Mr. Roy Fleming of Ottawa and were called to my attention by Dr. Fred Landon.

2. Statistics on Vessels Stranded*

Vessel	Gross Tonnage	Length Over All	Beam	When Built	Estimated Damage to Ship	Lives Lost	Location of Stranding	Owner
Acadian	2305	266.5'	43'	1908	$30,000		Thunder Bay, Lake Huron	Merchants Mutual Line Ltd., Toronto
A. E. Stewart	3943	376'	50'	1902	30,000		Thunder Bay, Lake Huron	Stewart Transportation Co., John J. Barlum, Mgr., Detroit
Barges					100,000		Cleveland Harbor, Lake Erie	Pittsburgh Steamship Co., Cleveland
D. O. Mills	6598	552'	58'	1907	45,000		Harbor Beach, Lake Huron	Interlake Steamship Co., Cleveland
F. G. Hartwell	6223	524'	58'	1908	30,000		Iroquois Light, Lake Superior	Mutual Steamship Co., G. A. Tomlinson, Mgr., Cleveland
Fulton	4219	444'	46'	1896	2,500		Bar Point, Lake Erie	Pittsburgh Steamship Co., Cleveland
G. J. Grammer	4471	454'	48'	1902	1,500		Lorain Harbor, Lake Erie	Seither Transit Co., W. H. Becker, Mgr., Cleveland
H. B. Hawgood	4655	434'	50'	1903	7,000		Weis Beach, Lake Huron	Acme Transit Co., Hawgood & Co., Mgr., Cleveland
Huronic	3330	328'	43'	1902	30,000		Whitefish Point, Lake Superior	Northern Navigation Co., Sarnia, Ontario
J. M. Jenks	4644	434'	50'	1902	25,000		Midland Harbor, Georgian Bay	Acme Transit Co., Hawgood & Co., Mgr., Cleveland
J. T. Hutchinson	3734	366'	48'	1901	40,000		Point Iroquois, Lake Superior	Pioneer Steamship Co., Hutchinson & Co., Mgr., Cleveland

2. Statistics on Vessels Stranded (Cont.)

Vessel	Gross Tonnage	Length Over All	Beam	When Built	Estimated Damage to Ship	Lives Lost	Location of Stranding	Owner
Matthew Andrews	7014	552'	56'	1907	2,500		Corsica Shoal, Lake Huron	Kinsman Transit Co., H. Steinbrenner, Mgr., Cleveland
Meaford	1889	268.5'	42'	1903	500		St. Marys River	Farrar Transportation Co., Ltd., Collingwood, Ontario
Northern Queen	2476	319'	40.5'	1888	25,000		Kettle Point, Lake Huron	Mutual Transit Co., Buffalo
Pontiac	2298	320'	40'	1889	7,500		Simmon's Reef, Straits of Mackinac	Cleveland-Cliffs Iron Co., Cleveland
Saxona	4716	436'	50'	1903	1,500		Lake St. Clair	Zenith Steamship Co., Cleveland
Scottish Hero	2201	317'	40'	1895	500		Lake Superior	Merchants Mutual Line, Ltd., Toronto
Victory	4527	472'	48'	1895	12,000		Livingstone Channel, Detroit River	Interlake Steamship Co., Cleveland
W. G. Pollock	4872	440'	52'	1906	5,000		Lake St. Clair	Valley Steamship Co., W. H. Becker, Mgr., Cleveland
Wm. Nottingham	4234	400'	50'	1902	75,000	3	Parisian Island, Lake Superior	Great Lakes Steamship Co., Cleveland

* Source: Lake Carriers' Association *Annual Report, 1913* (Cleveland, 1913).

3. Locations of Storm Damage*

Waters on Which Disasters Occurred	Number of Vessels	Tonnage	Value of Vessels and Cargoes Combined	Total Value of Property Lost	Lives Lost
Lake Huron	24	91,000	$5,199,000	$2,584,400	188
Lake Erie	17	51,028	1,521,500	143,500	6
Lake Michigan	16	28,958	1,597,500	459,500	10
Lake Superior	10	36,500	1,475,000	944,500	44
Straits of Mackinac	1	2,300	117,000	15,000	
Detroit River	2	8,700	471,000	10,000	
St. Marys River	1	1,900	†	500	
Total	71	220,486	10,381,000	4,157,400	248

* Source: *Annual Report of the United States Life-Saving Service for the Fiscal Year Ended June 30, 1914* (Washington: Government Printing Office, 1914), p. 28. About these figures, the Life-Saving Service reports, "It is obviously impossible to present a complete reckoning of the number of lives and the value of the property lost in this storm. Some of the vessels involved were of foreign registry, concerning which duly authenticated information is not readily obtainable. Moreover, numerous vessels of American registry doubtless sustained damage amounting to less than $300, a loss which their owners would not be required under the law to report. Neither are any figures available showing the extent of the loss sustained by undocumented vessels, such as gasoline launches, rowboats, and other small craft, of which there must have been a large number both damaged and destroyed, and doubtless lives were lost from aboard some of them as well. It may be assumed, however, that the figures given in this account are approximately correct with respect to the class of vessels to which they refer."
† British steamer *Meaford,* value of vessel and cargo unknown.

APPENDIX B

1. Cross Section of a Modern Standard 600-Foot Great Lakes Bulk Freighter

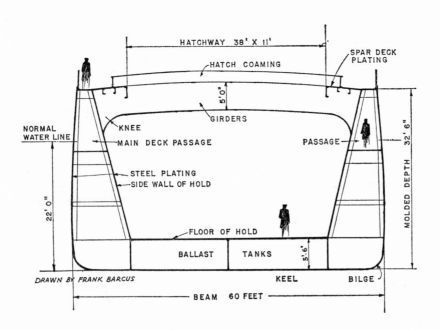

2. Cross Section of a Modern Standard 600-Foot Great Lakes Bulk Freighter

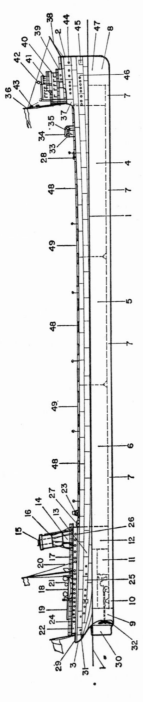

Length 610′ 9″   **Beam 60′**

Gross Tonnage 8245

Net Tons 6127

DRAWN BY FRANK BARCUS

1. Normal Water Line 22′
2. Stem
3. Stern
4. Hold No. 1, 147′ Long
5. Hold No. 2, 144′ Long
6. Hold No. 3, 147′ Long
   Total Length 438′,
   Total Capacity 579,640 Cu. Ft.
7. Ballast Tanks—9 on Each Side of Keel,
   Total Capacity 7880 Tons of Water
8. Forepeak Tank, 400 Tons
9. After Peak Tank, 102 Tons
10. Bilge Well
11. Propelling Machinery: Turbines, Condensers, and Stokers
12. Boilers, 450 Lbs. Per Sq. In.
13. Coal Bunker, 282 Tons
14. Soot Blower
15. Inner Stack
16. Outer Stack
17. Coal Bunker Hatch
18. Two 22′ 6″ Lifeboats, 25 Persons Each
19. Two 3000 Gal. Water Tanks
20. 1000 Gal. Drinking Water Tank
21. 702 Gal. Fuel Oil Tank
22. After Deck House
23. Traveling Gantry Crane for Hatch Covers
24. Spar Deck Aft—Diesel and Generator, Dining Room, Galley, Mess Room, Crew's
    Rooms (9), Baths (8)
25. Main Deck Aft—Machines, Generators, Machine Shop
26. Bulwark
27. Mooring Winches (2)
28. Mooring Winches (2)
29. Mooring Winch
30. Rudder Plate
31. 6000 Lb. Stern Anchor
32. Solid Bronze Propeller, 15′ 6″ Diameter
33. Forward Deck House—Private Dining
    Room, Galley
34. 450 Gal. Drinking Water Tank
35. Life Raft, 25 Persons
36. Foremast
37. Spar Deck Forward—Forward Crew Rooms
    (4), Baths (3)
38. Bowsprit
39. Forecastle Deck—Guest Rooms (2), Baths
    (2)
40. Upper Deck—Observation Room, Captain's
    Office, Room, Bath
41. Pilot House and Chart Room
42. Radio Direction-Finder
43. Signal Lamps
44. Windlass Room, Mooring Winch
45. Two 8000 Lb. Bower Anchors, Hoist Speed
    25 Ft. Per Minute, 180 Fathoms 2¼″ Steel
    Link Chain, also 350 Ft. 1″ Dia. Wire
    Hawser, and 70 Ft. 1¼″ Wire Hawser
46. Main Deck Forward—Crew's Sitting Room,
    Deck Hands' Rooms (6), Baths (3)
47. Dunnage Deck, Boiler, Stoker, Paint Room
48. 18 Hatches, Each 38′ x 11′, 13′ of Deck
    Between Hatches
49. Wire Rope Railing, 3 Lines

APPENDIX C

1. Extract from "Climatological Data for November, 1913, District No. 4, The Lake Region"

by J. H. Armington, Acting District Editor *

Storm of November 7–10

The storm of the 7th to 10th was one of the severest that has ever crossed the Lake Region. While higher winds have been recorded in connection with other disturbances, the velocities experienced in this storm were at most stations far above the verifying limits for windstorms, and they continued so long as to cause extraordinarily high seas which swept the Lakes with tremendous force. Many disasters and casualties occurred as a result of the storm. Breakwaters were broken up, and banks on the windward shores were badly washed out. The disturbance was accompanied over the central and eastern portions of the lakes by driving snow, which increased the precarious situation of vessels, tied up land traffic, and caused much damage to a considerable distance from the shore.

Owing to the exceptional severity of this storm, reports of various Weather Bureau officials relative to it are given in considerable detail:

> *Duluth, Minn.*—There was no loss of life or vessel property on the extreme western end of Lake Superior as a result of the great storm which passed over the Lake Region on the 7th to 10th, but some local damage occurred to property ashore in sections near the Duluth-Superior harbor during the northwest gale which prevailed on the afternoon and evening of the 7th. During this storm the maximum velocities ranged anywhere from 34 to 62 miles between 1 p. m.

* *Monthly Weather Review*, November 1913, pp. 1678–1680.

and 7 p. m., its intensity being greatest about 7 p. m. and ceasing abruptly a few minutes after the latter hour. This was the only blow of any consequence during the month.— H. W. Richardson, Duluth, Minn.

Sault Ste. Marie, Mich.—The storm of the 7th to 10th was the most severe experienced on the lakes for many years. A large fleet anchored in the upper river and the lower part of White Fish Bay. The wind and sea sweeping down the bay, into the river, caused the steamers *J. C. Hutchinson* and *Fred G. Hartwell* to drag their anchors and strike rock shoals, sinking both vessels and causing very heavy damage. The steamer *William Nottingham* struck a shoal near White Fish Point and was very badly damaged. Three of the crew were drowned while trying to reach shore in a small boat. The steamer *Cornell* was in the gale above White Fish Point from Friday morning until Monday night. She sustained very heavy damage and was kept off the beach only with the greatest difficulty. Other disasters occurred farther up the lake. While the wind at this station reached a maximum velocity of only 37 NW. at 6.55 p. m. on the 9th, vessel-masters report that on the open lake it was 60 to 80 miles per hour. A very peculiar feature was reported by Capt. Noble, steamer *Cornell*. About midnight of Thursday, the 6th, while on the course from White Fish Point to Keweenaw, and about 50 miles west of the point, with the wind light from the southeast, he suddenly encountered an unusually high northwest sea, and shortly afterward the wind backed to northerly, blowing a gale, which lasted until Monday night. The Canadian steamer *Leafield,* loaded with steel rails, for Port Arthur, has not been heard from since leaving Sault Ste. Marie, Ontario. The fine steel steamer *Henry B. Smith* left Marquette Sunday evening, the 9th, and has never been heard of. The steel steamer *L. C. Waldo* was driven on Manitou Island and will probably prove a total loss. The Canadian steamer *Turret Chief* was driven on Keweenaw Point and will probably prove a total loss. The crews of the *Waldo* and *Turret Chief* suffered great hardships before being rescued. Gales reaching a velocity of 46 to 48 miles on the 23d and 24th caused vessels to remain in shelter.—Alexander G. Burns. Sault Ste. Marie, Mich.

The storm on Lake Huron on November 9, 1913.—The storm of November 9 will be entered in the history of navigation as one of the most violent and one that exacted a greater toll of life and property on Lake Huron than any other storm within memory of local navigators. After its fury had subsided, it was found that 8 boats were missing, some of which ranked with the best on the lakes, and with them went down 200 lives. Ten boats were stranded, of which 2 were abandoned as total loss, while the others were released in more or less damaged condition. The greatest casualties occurred on the southern part of the lake, presumably within a hundred miles of Port Huron. Here 9 out of the 10 boats were stranded, and all the 8 missing boats are supposed to have foundered. Most of the stranded boats were found near the entrance to Saginaw Bay, between Port Austin and Harbor Beach, Mich.

The survivors' accounts of the storm and of their struggle to keep their vessels afloat are almost heart-rending. The water, they claim, was simply a seething mass, such as they have never seen before. So helplessly were they tossed about by the waves and carried by the currents that most of them did not know where they were. Some of those that were stranded near Saginaw Bay felt absolutely sure before striking ground that they were at least 10 to 15 miles from the shore, others again were under the impression that they were near the middle of the lake, somewhere opposite Sturgeon Point.

The story of the struggle of the 8 vessels that were lost in Lake Huron will never be known, neither are the places known where 7 of them foundered. The bodies of some of the crews, as well as considerable wreckage, were washed ashore on the Canadian side of the lake, all along between Kincardine and Kettle Point, so the natural supposition is that the boats were lost in the lower half of the lake.

One of the foundered boats, the *Charles S. Price,* was discovered 11 miles north of Port Huron and 7 miles offshore completely turned over. Her hull protruded about 20 feet above the water when she was first discovered, evidently buoyed up by the imprisoned air that was bubbling up all around her. She settled gradually and disappeared under the water on the 17th of November. Some of the bodies were washed ashore near Goderich, Ontario, about 55 miles northeast from where she sank.

The storm began on this part of the lake about 6 a. m. of the 9th, when the wind became brisk northwest. The first verifying velocity (36 miles) occurred at 9.50 a. m., and from that time to 1.30 p. m. the wind increased very little but fluctuated between 20 and 42 miles per hour. About 1.30 p. m. it shifted to the north, and increased steadily until it attained an extreme velocity of 62 miles per hour, at 9.02 p. m. A comparison with the wind record from Harbor Beach,

TABLE I—*Casualties on Lake Huron during storm of November 9, 1913*

STEAMERS FOUNDERED

Name	Lives lost	Value of steamer	Value of cargo
Charles S. Price	28	$325,583	$21,768
John A. McGean	23	225,000	18,000
Isaac M. Scott	28	325,158	21,961
Argus	24	155,000	30,000
Hydrus	23	155,000	20,000
Regina	22	[1] 100,000	....
Wexford	22	[1] 80,000	....
James Carruthers	30	[1] 375,000	....
Total	200	1,740,741	111,729

[1] Approximate value

STEAMERS STRANDED

Name	Location	Value of steamer	Value of cargo lost	Remarks
Matthew Andrews	Port Edward ...	....	None....	Released
H. B. Hawgood	...do..........	....	None....	Do.
D. O. Mills	Harbor Beach ..	....	....	Do.
Rhoda Emily	...do..........	....	....	Do.
Edward Buckly	...do..........	....	....	Do.
Northern Queen	Kettle Point ...	....	....	Do.
J. M. Jenks	Midland	....	....	Do.
Acadian	Alpena	....	....	Do.
Matoa	Point aux Barques	$123,600	$7,000	Abandoned
Howard M. Hanna, jr. .	Port Austin ...	325,000	20,000	Do.

Mich., near the entrance to Saginaw Bay, shows that the wind was nearly the same in that part of the lake also. The highest and steadiest winds occurred between 6 and 10 p. m., and that was the time when most of the accidents occurred. Even the watches that were found on the dead bodies were stopped between 8 and 11.30, and probably indicated the time when the boats went to pieces and the sailors entered their watery graves.

The station barometer began to fall about 2 a. m. of the 9th, when it stood near 29.70 inches sea level, and reached the lowest point, 28.95 sea level, at 8 p. m. During the fall the wind was strong from the northwest and north, indicating that the storm was increasing in energy, as its center was already east of the station.

The damage on land and along the shore, although considerable and will probably total over $100,000 in Port Huron alone, appears insignificant when compared with the losses on the open lake. Telegraph and telephone communication was crippled for several days. Trains and electric cars were stalled by the blinding snowstorm, which piled up the snow in drifts 4 to 5 feet high. A few store windows were smashed in, and several houses were unroofed. The water rose 4 to 5

TABLE II—*Hourly maximum wind velocities at Port Huron, Mich.*

Hours	Velocity	Hours	Velocity
November 9, p. m.:	*Miles*	November 9, p. m.—Continued	*Miles*
1–2	40	9–10	56
2–3	40	10–11	50
3–4	46	11–12	46
4–5	47	November 10, a. m.:	
5–6	52	12–1	45
6–7	56	1–2	42
7–8	58	2–3	40
8–9	56	3–4	38

feet above normal height at the foot of the lake and in St. Clair River, and caused considerable damage to shops and dock property along the water front. The Fort Gratiot lighthouse at the foot of the lake was badly undermined by the action of the waves, and the lightship, about 2 miles farther up in the lake, was torn loose from her anchorage and dragged with its occupants to the Canadian shore.—A. Wiesner, Port Huron, Mich.

At Cleveland, Ohio.—The unusual character and severity, in some respects, of the storm, together with the attendant appalling losses, were such as to warrant the prediction that it will go down in local history and be referred to for years to come as the "Great storm of November, 1913." For this reason a detailed though inadequate account of this storm, as experienced in Cleveland and vicinity, may be of interest. Coming so early in the season and combining as it did the chief features of the windstorm, the snowstorm, the ice storm, and the cold wave, it swept down upon the almost wholly unprepared city with well-nigh paralyzing effect. Discomfort, not to say actual suffering, was very general, although fortunately brief.

The storm proper may be said to have commenced in Cleveland about 4.30 a. m., Sunday, November 9, and to have ended about 2 p. m. Tuesday, November 11, as those dates mark the beginning and the ending of precipitation. The precipitation was at first mostly rain and very light but mixed with a small amount of very moist snow. By 10 a. m., however, the rain had entirely ceased and the snowfall had become heavy, being still quite moist. The snow continued heavy until the afternoon or evening of the 10th when it became light and so continued until about 2 p. m. of the 11th. The total amount of snowfall, unmelted, during the entire storm was 22.2 inches, which melted gave 3.18 inches of water. The greatest amount of snowfall in any 24 hours during the storm was 17.4 inches between 7 p. m. of the 9th and 7 p. m. of the 10th. The greatest previous 24-hour fall since the opening of the station in 1870 was 13 inches on February 9, 1896.

At the beginning of the storm the temperature was about 36°, gradually falling during the day to slightly below 30°, remaining about stationary during the 10th and 11th, and falling to about 20° on the morning of the 12th. The storm set in with a moderate northwest wind that steadily increased, reaching the verifying velocity (40 miles per hour) about 1.50 p. m. of the 9th. From 2 p. m. of the 9th until 6 a. m. of the 10th the wind blew with a remarkably uniform velocity, the total movement during those 16 hours being 779 miles, or an average velocity of about 49 miles per hour. The highest or maximum velocity attained was only 62 miles at 4.40 p. m. of the 9th, and the extreme was 79 miles at about the same time. The wind continued quite constantly from the northwest up to 2 p. m. of the 9th when it showed a tendency to shift to the west but continued to vacillate between northwest and west until about 7.30 p. m. when it shifted definitely and permanently to the west, from which direction it came until about 8.20 a. m. of the 10th when it went to the southwest and so continued to the end of the storm.

At the beginning of the storm, the barometer showed a pressure of about 29.60 inches, decreasing rather rapidly. The lowest reading of the barometer as shown by the barograph trace was about 29.07 inches and occurred between 9 and 10 a. m. of the 9th, after which time the pressure rose, quite rapidly at first, until the end of the storm.

As stated already, the temperatures at the beginning of the storm were so near the freezing point as to make conditions decidedly favorable for the formation of ice and the heavy deposit of snow on wires, tree trunks, limbs, etc., so that by Sunday night all telegraph and telephone wires, electric-light wires, trolley wires, trees, etc., were incased in ice and so heavily burdened with snow that under the pressure of a 50-mile gale, poles and wires began to break and fall in every direction, trees either broke or were weighted to the ground, so that the telephone, telegraph, trolley, and electric-light services were completely paralyzed or seriously crippled and all traffic greatly demoralized. The extent of the losses can not be ascertained even approximately at this time but will be very large here in Cleveland. The loss of life in this city was small.—William H. Alexander, Cleveland, Ohio.

Buffalo, N. Y.—The dominating feature of the weather for the month of November, 1913, was the destructive storm that caused widespread disaster over the Great Lakes from the 7th to the 10th, inclusive. The storm center passed this station between 6 and 7 p. m. of the 9th and caused an unusually low reading of the barometer here, the lowest reading being 28.69 inches reduced to sea level.

Moderately heavy rain and only moderate to brisk northerly and easterly winds prevailed here on the 9th. At 3.30 a. m. of the 10th the wind became high from the south and from that hour until 5 p. m. a gale, accompanied by heavy snow, raged over this city, the highest velocity, 80 miles from the southwest, occurring at 1.17 p. m. Notwithstanding the gale averaged over 60 miles an hour from 7 a. m. to 4 p. m., there were no casualties at this end of Lake Erie, except that of lightship *No. 82*, which was lost with a crew of six men. The lightship was stationed off Point Abino, about 13 miles from Buffalo. Several small pleasure yachts were driven on the beach at the Buffalo Yacht Club. The small loss to the shipping interests in this section was unquestionably due to timely warnings issued by the bureau, for a large fleet of steamers remained in port until the storm subsided. More than 30 large steamers were back of the outer break-water waiting for an opportunity to go out, and their esti-mated value is close to $1,000,000. The heavy moist snow that fell on the 10th impeded traffic here somewhat. In fact, I am of the opinion that if the gale that raged over the Lakes from the 8th to 10th, inclusive, had not been accompanied by heavy snow the loss of life would have been small and few, if any, boats would probably have been wrecked, as the storm was no record breaker for wind in this section.

Compared with other storms, particularly those that have occurred in November, we find that the gale on November 21, 1900, was of longer duration and much more destructive in this locality. Damage to the amount of $300,000 was done to the breakwaters by this storm and the shipping interests suffered a loss of $100,000. The maximum velocity for this storm was 80 miles from the southwest against 80 miles from the southwest in the recent storm, but the 80 miles in Novem-ber, 1900, was at an elevation of 206 feet, while the 80 miles during the recent storm was at an elevation of 279 feet, which would make the former about 15 per cent higher. The verify-ing velocity was raised from 46 miles on the Prudential Build-ing to 54 miles on the Telephone Building, the present loca-tion of the local offices.—D. Cuthbertson, Buffalo, N. Y.

2. Extracts from U. S. Department of Agriculture, Weather Bureau, "Daily Local Record," November 7-11, 1913

Friday, November 7, Notes

Storm Warning: "Hoist southwest storm warning 10:00 a.m. Storm over upper Mississippi valley moving northeast. Brisk to high southwest winds this afternoon and tonight, shifting to north-west Saturday on upper Lakes. Warnings ordered throughout Great Lakes." Received 9:29 a.m. and disseminated by map, tele-phone, display and newspapers.

Saturday, November 8, Notes

Storm Warning: "Change to northwest storm warning 10:00 a.m. Storm over eastern Lake Superior moving east-northeast. High west to northwest winds." Received 9:30 a.m. and disseminated by map, telephone, display and newspapers.

Sunday, November 9, Notes

Storm Warning: "Continue northwest storm warning. Storm over Virginia moving northeast." Received 10:15 a.m. and disseminated by Captain Card, telephone and newspapers.

The press reports four ships driven ashore or on rocks, viz.: "Louisiana" off Port Washington, Wisconsin; "Mary" aground near Algonac; unidentified ship on Point Pelee, Lake Erie; "Mary Elphicke" on Bar Point (aground). [*Tribune*]

Monday, November 10, Notes

Storm Warning: "Continue northwest storm warning 10:00 a.m." Received 9:10 a.m. and disseminated by map, telephone and newspapers. The daily press (*Free Press*) reports the following: "Steamer Pollock (thought to be) blown ashore above ship canal at St. Clair Flats. Forty vessels driven to anchor in St. Clair and Detroit rivers. Fifty reported anchored in Thunder Bay. Fifty more reported as finding refuge between 'Soo' and White Fish Point."

Tuesday, November 11, Notes

The daily press of today (*Free Press*) reports the following: "Steamer D. C. Perry blown from its moorings at Holland, Michigan and swept on the beach. Unidentified freighter turns turtle eight miles north Port Huron. Steamer James E. Davidson is reported sunk off Groscap Point. Wreckage from steamer L. C. Waldo is carried ashore near Big Bay, north Keeweenaw."

A Glossary of Nautical Terms

Aft—Towards, at, or near the stern.

After End—The stern.

Alee—Toward or on the lee side. "To put the helm alee"—to bring the helm toward the side of the ship away from the wind, thus heading the ship into the wind.

Amidships—Half way between bow and stern.

Anchorage—A place where a ship may anchor, especially a particular section of a harbor.

Astarboard—Toward or on the starboard side. "To put the helm astarboard"—To bring the helm toward the side of the ship toward the wind, thus heading the ship away from the wind.

Athwartship—Across the ship at right angles to the keel.

Auxiliaries—Machinery that is supplementary to the main operating units.

Ballast—Any weight, usually water, carried to keep the ship from becoming top heavy, or to change her trim in order to counterbalance the effect of the wind.

Ballast Tank—A watertight compartment for holding ballast.

Barge—A ship or vessel that has no power or sail and must be towed; a flat-bottomed craft.

Batten—A strip of wood used to fasten the edge of a tarpaulin to a hatch coaming.

Beam—The broadest width of a ship.

Bilge—The rounded lower portion of a hull; the recess in the bottom of the ship into which all water drains.

Binnacle—A case or stand containing the ship's compass and a lamp for night use.

Bitt—A vertical post used in making lines fast.

Boat Deck—A deck on which lifeboats are kept.

Boatswain *or* Bos'n—The officer of a ship who is in charge of rigging, anchors, etc.

Boilerhouse—A passageway above the boilers and immediately under the smokestack.

Bow—The extreme forward end of a ship.

Breakwater *or* Breakwall—A concrete or stone pier usually for breaking the force of waves to protect a harbor or launching area.

Breeches Buoy—A device used in lifesaving, consisting of a pair of short-legged canvas breeches hanging from a cork life preserver which encloses the person to be rescued, attached to a rope which is stretched from one ship to another or from ship to shore and is drawn forward by hauling lines.

Bulkhead—A partition that separates one part of a ship from another part.

Bulwark—A part of the ship's side extending above the deck.

Bunker—A compartment for stowing coal or other fuel.

Buoy—A caution marker for a channel.

Buoyancy—The ability to float. The distribution of weight within a vessel will either increase or decrease its buoyancy.

Cabin—A room in a ship for officers or passengers.

Cable—A rope or chain by which an anchor is attached to a ship.

Catspaw—A hitch in a rope so made as to form two eyes into which a tackle may be hooked.

Centerboard—A broad board or slab of wood or metal amidships, pivoted at the forward lower corner so that it may be raised in shallow water or when the ship is beached, or lowered to increase resistance and prevent wind reaction.

Centerline—An imaginary line dividing the ship in half longitudinally.

Chadburn—A telegraph device used to signal from the bridge to the engine room.

Chain Pipe—A pipe through which an anchor chain is passed from the deck to a stowage compartment.

Chock—A heavy iron fitting through which a rope or hawser is passed.

Coaming—The vertical edge of a hatch or skylight.

Coast Guard (U.S.)—An organization created by act of Congress,

January 28, 1915, by a merger of the U.S. Revenue Cutter Service with the U.S. Lifesaving Service.

Compass—An instrument for finding directions. The most commonly used type on the Great Lakes is the magnetic liquid compass. The liquid (45% alcohol, 55% distilled water) is in a bronze bowl in which the compass card rests, sealed by a thick, watertight plate-glass cover. The liquid reduces oscillations of the card, making the compass easier to read in a heavy seaway.

Compass Card—A circular card, marked off into 360 degrees, attached to the needle of a mariner's compass.

Compass Point—*See* Point.

Coston Flare *or* Coston Signal—A flare or rocket for use at night as a distress signal.

Deadlight—A strong shutter on a port or cabin window that keeps out water.

Deck—The flat upper surface of a ship.

Deck House—A shelter built on deck.

Deep Sounding Lead—A lead weighing from 30 to 100 pounds, attached to a line of 100 or more fathoms.

Derelict—A ship adrift at sea without her crew.

Down Bound—Traveling with the current; on the Great Lakes, from the northern lakes toward the southern lakes.

Draft—The distance from the water line to the bottom of the hull; the depth of water necessary to float a ship.

Draw Water—To sink in water to a certain depth.

Fantail—The stern overhang of a vessel.

Fathom—Six feet; used in measuring the depth of water by sounding.

Fetch Up—To hold in place; to catch hold; to run aground.

Firehold—A compartment in the lower part of the vessel where the firemen work.

Fore-and-Aft—In a line with the length of the ship; longitudinally.

Foremast—The mast nearest the bow.

Forepeak—A large compartment just aft of the bow in the lower part of the ship, used for trimming ship.

Foreward *or* For'd—At, near, or towards the bow of the ship.

Funnel—The smokestack of a vessel.

Galley—The kitchen of a ship.

Gas Buoy—A metal buoy filled with compressed illuminating gas, having on top a lantern that burns night and day.

Gross Tonnage—The total internal capacity of a ship, reckoned at 100 cubic feet per ton.

Gunwale—The upper edge of the side of a ship.

Gyro-compass—A mechanical compass operated by means of a gyroscope, and indicating true north rather than magnetic north.

Halyard—A rope by which a flag, sail or yard is hoisted.

Hatch—The cover for a hatchway.

Hatchway—An opening in a deck leading below.

Hawse Pipe—A large fitting or casting extending from the deck to the side of a ship near the bow, through which the anchor chain passes.

Hawser—A large rope used in towing or mooring.

Helm—The apparatus for steering a ship. "Answer the helm"—To respond to changes in the direction of the helm.

Helmsman—A wheelsman.

Hold—The space inside a vessel where cargo or supplies are carried.

Hull—The body of a ship, including framing, decks, bulkheads, stanchions, keel and floors.

Hurricane Deck—An upper deck not intended to support much weight.

Inboard—Inside the ship; towards the center of the ship.

Keel—The principal fore-and-aft structural member of a ship's frame, formed of flat plates laid end to end, and extending from stem to stern on the centerline along the bottom of the ship; the backbone of a ship.

Keelson—A fore-and-aft member which strengthens the keel.

Lead—A weight attached to a line for use in sounding.

Lead Line—A line to which a lead is attached for sounding depths at sea.

Lee—The side of a ship away from the direction of the wind. Also, a shore on the lee side of a ship, and therefore to be feared, for the force of the wind tends to blow the ship ashore. "Under the lee of the shore"—In the shelter of a shore line from which the wind is blowing.

Leeward—On the lee side.

Length Over All (L.O.A.)—The length of a ship from the stem to the aftermost point of the stern.

Life Belt—A life preserver in the form of a belt.

Lifeboat—A boat carried on a ship or maintained ashore for saving lives in case of shipwreck.

Life Buoy—A ring of canvas-covered cork, usually fitted with loops or rope and designed to be thrown to a person who has fallen overboard to keep him afloat until rescued. It is usually carried on the rail for immediate use.

Lifeline—A line attached to a vessel to be clung to or to make it easier to reach the ship; also, a line stretched along a deck to be clung to, especially during storms.

Life Preserver—A buoyant canvas vest which will keep a person afloat. *See* Life Buoy.

Life Raft—A floating device for saving lives in case of shipwreck, having room for a number of persons and taking the place of a lifeboat. Life rafts are usually made of air-filled metal cylinders, and are preferred to lifeboats because they take up less room on board ship.

Liferail—A handrail on the sides of the cabins to be clung to in heavy weather.

Lifesaver—A member of the Lifesaving Service.

Lifesaving Service (U.S.)—An organization established in 1871 under the direction of the Treasury Department, organized into a separate bureau in 1878, and merged into the U.S. Coast Guard in 1915.

Light—Carrying little or no cargo.

Lighter—To transport goods to or on a lighter, a large open barge.

Lighthouse Service—(1910–39) An organization created by Act of Congress for carrying out the design, construction and maintenance of all lighthouses, wharves, depots, and other fixed structures.

Lightship—A floating lighthouse, securely moored where it will mark a danger, such as a reef, or at the entrance of a harbor to show the safe way in.

Line—A small rope.

List—To lean over to one side. A leaning to one side.

Lock—An enclosure in a canal or river with gates at each end, used in raising or lowering ships as they pass from one water level to another.

Lock at the Soo—To pass up or down through the locks at Sault Ste. Marie.

Log—A record of a ship's daily progress; a nautical record. Also, an apparatus, originally a piece of wood, trailed behind a ship for measuring the ship's rate of speed. The mechanical type is also called a *patent log.*

Loggy—Heavy; lacking buoyancy; hard to maneuver.

Mariner—A sailor.

Mast—The large round piece of timber or steel tube standing nearly vertical at the centerline of the ship on deck, for supporting rigging, wireless antennae, halyards, etc.

Master—The commander or captain of a ship; the skipper.

Mate—A deck officer ranking below the captain; the master's assistant.

Messroom—The dining room of a ship.

Midships—Amidships.

Mile—The statute mile (5280 feet) rather than the nautical mile is used for measuring distance on the Great Lakes.

Molded Depth—The distance from the top of the keel to the top of the upper deck amidships.

Moor—To secure a ship in position by several lines or cables.

Mushroom Anchor—An anchor, shaped like a mushroom, capable of grasping the ground however it falls; used chiefly for permanent moorings.

Oiler—A seaman whose job it is to oil the ship's machinery.

Overhang—The portion of the hull hanging over and unsupported by the water.

Pier—A long narrow structure of wood, steel, or concrete, built from the shore out into the water and used for transfer of passengers and cargo between ship and shore.

Pig Boat—A ship with a bow shaped like a pig's snout; a whaleback.

Pilot House *or* Wheel House—An enclosed place in which the main steering wheel, controls, engine room telegraph, etc. are located.

Point—One of 32 equal divisions of the compass card, each point containing 11 degrees, 15 minutes of arc.

Port—The left-hand side of the ship when looking forward. A harbor. A port hole.

Port Hole—A circular opening or window in a ship's side. Also called a *sidelight*.

Powerhouse—The area where mechanical or electrical power is generated.

Propeller—The screw-like revolving device, usually having three or four blades and similar to an electric fan in appearance, which drives the ship through the water.

Quadrant—An instrument for measuring altitudes.

Quarterdeck—A deck toward the stern of a ship, usually used by the officers.

Quarters—Living or sleeping rooms for officers and crew.

Rail—The upper edge of the bulwarks.

Rigging—Hemp or wire ropes or lashings used to support booms, masts, spars, etc.

Roll—The motion of the ship from side to side, alternately raising and lowering each side of the deck.

Rudder—A large movable surface at the stern by which the ship is steered.

Schooner—A sailing vessel having two fore-and-aft rigged masts.

Scupper—A drain for running off water, as from the edge of a deck overboard.

Shaft—A round, heavy forging that connects the engine to the propeller.

Shell—The outside plating of a ship from stem to stern.

Ship Water—To take in water, as through a leak or break.

Soo—Sault Sainte Marie.

Sounding—The measurement of depth by a lead weight attached to a line, operated mechanically or by hand.

Spar—A mast, yard, or boom, usually round, made of wood or metal.

Spar Deck—The upper deck of a ship.

Stack—The smokestack of a ship.

Stanchion—An upright member used as a support between decks.

Starboard *or* Starb'd—The right-hand side of the ship when looking forward.

Steerageway—The rate of motion sufficient to make a ship answer its helm.

Steering Gear—Apparatus for controlling the rudder.

Steersman—A wheelsman.

Stem—The extreme bow of the ship extending the full height from keel to top deck.

Stern—The after end of a ship.

Strong-back—A heavy timber or bar.

Superstructure—Deck houses and other structures above the weather deck.

Surfman—A person skilled in handling a boat in surf; especially, a member of the Lifesaving Service.

Tarpaulin—A waterproof canvas covering.

Telegraph—A mechanically or electrically operated means of signalling from the bridge to the engine room.

Tender—A vessel used to assist other vessels, as in supplying provisions.

Texas—The structure on the upper deck of a steamer containing officers' cabins, etc., with the pilot house in front or on top.

Tiller—An arm attached to a rudder head for operating the rudder.

Trim—To shift ballast; to cause a ship to change its position in the water. Also, the way a ship rests in the water.

Trough—A hollow or depression between waves.

Turn Turtle—To capsize.

Up Bound—Traveling against the current; on the Great Lakes, from the southern lakes toward the northern lakes.

Ventilator—A device for furnishing fresh air to compartments below deck or for exhausting foul air.

Weather—The side of a ship toward the direction of the wind.

Weather Deck—A deck having no overhead protection.

Weigh Anchor—To lift the anchor from the bottom.

Whaleback—A ship that resembles the back of a whale, the main deck rounded over, waves passing completely over it without resistance or injury to the ship. Also called a *pig boat*.

Wheel Chain—A chain leading from the axis of the steering wheel to the tiller, for operating the rudder.

Wheelsman—A man whose job it is to steer a vessel.

Wildcat—A drum or wheel on a windlass having teeth which engage the links of the chain cable and thus regulate its speed.

Winch—A small hoisting engine.

Windlass—A machine used for hoisting anchors.

Windy Young—[This was evidently a device for securing a wooden hatch cover of the type commonly used in 1913, but I have been unable to obtain a description of it. The term probably went out of use when newer types of hatch covers made the device obsolete.]

Index

Edited by Georgiana Ward Strickland

Designed by Peter Gilleran
Set in Linotype Caledonia and Bulmer type faces
Printed on Warren's Olde Style Antique Wove paper
Bound in Bancroft Arrestox book cloth
Manufactured in the United States of America